Mobilizing Invisible Assets

Mobilizing
Invisible Assets

Hiroyuki Itami
with **Thomas W. Roehl**

Harvard University Press
Cambridge, Massachusetts
and London, England

Library of Congress Cataloging-in-Publication Data

Itami, Hiroyuki, 1945–
   Mobilizing invisible assets.

   Bibliography: p.
   Includes index.
   1. Strategic planning.   I. Roehl, Thomas W.
II. Title.   III. Title: Invisible assets.
HD30.28.I85   1987   658.4'012   86-26972
ISBN 0-674-57771-X (paper)

B42113037 X

Foreword
by Joseph L. Bower

In his diaries of the Second World War, General Sir Alan Brooke, the chief of the Imperial General Staff, reported his frustration with Winston Churchill's impetuousness. When Brooke urged Churchill to consider contingencies in advance, the prime minister would shake his fist in Brooke's face and say, "I do not want any of your long-term policies, they only cripple initiative."

For many observers of business today, this contrast between the systematic planner and the "true leader" exemplifies what is wrong with corporate strategy as a concept. Some have even argued for a theory of "emergent strategy," which might be interpreted as a kind of antiplanning. Noting how little time chief executives seem to spend on long-term planning and noting the success of companies that learn from experience, these authors assert that it is learning rather than "intended strategy" that accounts for the fine results.

In the same vein, the tenor of most discussions of Japanese management is anti–long-term planning. To highlight the clearly important roles of organization and culture in Japanese companies, the economic aspects of strategy and ex ante intent are relegated to secondary roles. In such books a Churchillian spirit and the innovativeness of a committed team are celebrated as the foundation of corporate excellence. Often portfolio theories of resource allocation are caricatured as a passing fad.

Treatments of corporate strategy that deal with systematic formulation and articulation of company purpose have been found wanting by many close observers of management. The phrasing of the prescription, calling for a close fit between company resources and the opportunities presented by a changing competitive environment, does not seem to correspond to the awkward incremental process by which strategy is actually developed. In a sense, the studies of strategy formulation and resource allocation have undermined the various normative theories of the process. The emphasis on organizational process and human psychology in descriptive studies seems to have diminished the role that analysis can or ought to play.

Hiroyuki Itami's book goes a long way to solving these problems. Written for Japanese managers, the book is a happy addition to the literature of management in the United States. By introducing a rich concept of "invisible assets," he provides an intuitively appealing way to recognize the vital contribution of accumulated experience and information to a corporation's strategic resources. Itami shows especially how commitment to a core concept of strategic purpose is reflected in invisible assets. His framework clarifies how corporate strategy, far from being a passive construct, is a necessity for a company that wishes to take advantage of technological change rather than be overtaken by it.

Itami's second important contribution is his emphasis on a dynamic fit between resources and the environment. He highlights the way in which the goals a leader sets forth for an organization should actually be *destabilizing*. If the goals are properly ambitious, the requirement that they be attainable forces the affected parts of the organization to grow and develop.

In this sense Itami has achieved something quite remarkable. With only a few additions to the vocabulary of conventional business economics, he has explained what it means to apply Robert Browning's famous adage of ambition—"a man's reach should exceed his grasp"—to corporations. The corporation that ignores this rule will die for lack of stimulus to achievement. In examining this somewhat romantic aim, Itami also explains many of the achievements of Japanese companies in the postwar period. This is especially important because so many treatments of Japan's national success focus on the triumph of the government's industrial and macroeconomic policies to the exclusion of the companies' strategies.

By treating the human assets of a business at length in strategic terms, Itami is able to emphasize the criticalness for corporate success of the operations and management work force. In an era when *Business Week* features "The End of Corporate Loyalty" as a cover story on the restructuring of American companies, Itami provides a framework that can help researchers and policy makers both in and out of business consider the necessity of investing in invisible assets—the knowledge, skills, and experience of committed people.

Preface

This is a book on the what and why of successful corporate strategies: what common characteristics they share and why there is a logic behind their success. Every strategist needs the answers to these questions, yet few books fill this need. Dozens of books on strategy formulation give the reader tools to analyze the environment and evaluate a firm's strengths. Such books discuss the how-to of strategy formulation, but have little to say about what and why. The lack of answers to these questions may reflect the tremendous variety of successful strategies. It is often believed that this degree of variation makes it impossible to find common themes in their content. I believe, however, that beneath the variety of strategies can be found a common strategic logic.

I do not mean that the architects of successful strategies have always used some formal analysis, nor do I claim that logical thinking assures strategic success. In many cases people arrive at successful strategies through intuition. They make the right decision on a hunch. Yet even in those cases one can see, in retrospect, a logic behind the success. It is possible to say why an intuitively conceived strategy worked so well. A born strategist does not require instruction in strategic logic, but the rest of us need this in advance, not in retrospect.

This book tries to systematically present strategic logic from a broad perspective. It deals not just with the logic of the market and of competition, but also with the logic of technology and human psychology in organizations. Strategy provides basic guidelines for corporate economic behavior as well as a unifying principle for a human organization. This holistic approach combines the analytical economic approach with the soft-behavioral one. Strategic logic needs both approaches.

In trying to distill and synthesize this logic, I have been heavily influenced by two different forms of analysis. One form, found in the strategy/corporate growth literature of the United States and Europe, includes the work of Edith Penrose on corporate growth, Kenneth Andrews on strategy, Igor Ansoff on diversification, Bruce Henderson on portfolio strategy, and Michael Porter on competitive strategy. The other source for my analysis is the vast array of examples of strategic success from Japanese companies. In fact, the book began as an effort to distill the common factors in Japanese competitive successes. In doing this, I arrived at the new concepts explained throughout the book: first, the invisible assets of a firm, which are based on information, and, second, overextension as an unbalanced growth strategy that stimulates resource accumulation and organizational vitality.

The reader will find many accounts of successful Japanese strategies here. Because I am most familiar with the strategies of Japanese firms, I draw on them frequently for examples. This does not mean that the logic applies only to Japanese business; it applies just as much to the United States. Strategic success knows no national boundaries.

This book was first published in Japan in 1980, then revised in 1984. This English translation is an adaptation of the revised edition. In preparing the original edition, I found the very stimulating research environment at Hitotsubashi University immensely instrumental. I thank Dean Ken'ichi Imai, Professor Tadao Miyakawa, and Professor Ikujiro Nonaka for providing that environment. My colleagues both at Hitotsubashi and elsewhere read drafts and gave me incisive comments. Among them I want to particularly acknowledge Hideki Yoshihara and Tadao Kagono of Kobe University; Hirotaka Takeuchi, Kiyonori Sakakibara, and Kunio Itoh of Hitotsubashi University; Professor Moriaki Tsuchiya of Tokyo University; and Akihiro Okumura of Keio University. Part of the research was done while I was visiting the Graduate School of Business at Stanford University. My special thanks go to Robert K. Jaedicke, Charles A. Holloway, and Steven Wheelwright.

Many Japanese business people contributed ideas and advice. Setsuya Tabuchi (chairman of the board, Nomura Securities) and Takao Igawa (executive vice president, Taio Paper) provided many insights on Japanese strategy. Among those who commented on the manuscript were Jiro Aoki (Matsushita Electric), Shinzo Katada (Nomura

Research Institute), Mitsuhiko Tanabe (Nomura Management School), and Toshiki Yokokawa (Oki Electric). Yoshitake Kurosawa, the editor of the Japanese edition, struggled along with me. Mariko Morita has been a most competent and cheerful assistant at Hitotsubashi.

Thomas Roehl of the University of Washington did an excellent translation and adaptation, combining his expertise in business economics and the Japanese language and adding many American examples. I was most fortunate to have the cooperation of someone of his caliber. He deserves to be noted as a collaborator for his vital contributions to this book. Roehl asks me to acknowledge the assistance of his wife, Junko, who was extremely helpful with the translation, using her knowledge of the two cultures to resolve seemingly irreconcilable differences between author and translator in how best to present ideas to an American audience. Student assistants Ted Klauber and Jim Hubbert were very helpful in editing the numerous drafts. Peg Anderson of Harvard University Press helped us present the ideas concisely and clearly, making the final text more readable.

Last, but certainly not least, I am deeply indebted to my family for their encouragement and patience with this irritable author. Alas, my wife, Michiko, and our sons, Kenichiro and Yujiro, had to go through the agony twice for this book, first for the Japanese edition and then for the English one.

Contents

The Concept of
Strategic Dynamics

Chapter 1

It is easy to observe strategic successes and failures in business. How can we learn from the successes and repeat them? What is the essence or logic behind them? This is the deceptively simple question this book addresses.

The essence of successful strategy lies in what I call *dynamic strategic fit,* the match over time between the factors that are external to a company (for example, customers' preferences) and the internal factors (for example, the firm's reputation for good service) and the content of strategy itself. Strategy must be consciously designed to fit these ever-changing factors. A firm achieves strategic fit through the effective use and efficient accumulation of its invisible assets, such as technological know-how or customer loyalty. Only a firm that carefully cultivates such assets will be in a position to achieve and maintain a record of successful strategy.

Analysts have tended to define assets too narrowly, identifying only those that can be measured, such as plant and equipment. Yet the intangible assets, such as a particular technology, accumulated consumer information, brand name, reputation, and corporate culture, are invaluable to the firm's competitive power. In fact, these invisible assets are often a firm's only real source of competitive edge that can be sustained over time. A firm that does not include technology among its assets cannot long remain competitive in this world of rapid technological innovation. If a firm has a reputation for high-quality products in one field, it can utilize its brand image to gain a head start over its competitors in a new product field. An active and creative corporate culture allows a company to overcome organizational obstacles when it embarks on a new business venture.

Given a firm's level of invisible assets, some strategies will work better than others. Previous decisions on invisible asset accumulation thus determine the set of strategies that can succeed in the short run. Some current strategies may not be fully supportable with the firm's current asset base, but it is dangerous to rule them out entirely. Current strategies may also be an efficient way to make valuable additions to the firm's invisible asset base, while careless utilization of this base can render the accumulated invisible assets, assembled at high cost, unusable in future strategic decisions. Current strategy, because it can change the level of invisible assets, is more than the basis for short-term competitive advantage; it lays the foundation for future strategy and adds to or erodes the invisible asset base.

The competitive success of a strategy is dependent on the firm's invisible assets, but the dynamics of invisible assets (their accumulation and depreciation over time) is also largely determined by the content of that strategy. This book explores how invisible assets affect and are affected by the firm's strategy. While the various environmental and internal factors of strategic fit will be discussed in turn, it is important to remember that invisible assets are the threads that bind together these strategic elements and help maintain and strengthen a firm's strategy over time.

Corporate Strategy Defined

Strategy is such a familiar term that it has become rather overused: anything that is important to the firm is considered strategic. Such a wide definition is unsuitable for analysis. In my more limited definition, strategy is what determines the framework of a firm's business activities and provides guidelines for coordinating activities so that the firm can cope with and influence the changing environment. Strategy articulates the firm's preferred relationships with its environment and the type of organization it is striving to become. Based on the influence each strategic decision has on the firm's activities—and, ultimately, on its performance—we can divide strategic decisions into two categories: fundamental and implementation. A decision to create a new product line is a fundamental strategy decision. A plan for carrying out such a decision—for example, how to price and advertise the new product—is an implementation decision. This book mostly concerns fundamental strategy, although many of the same strategic principles underlie implementation strategy as well.

It is customary in the literature on strategy to differentiate between corporationwide resource allocation decisions and division-level planning. The former is often called corporate strategy and the latter business strategy. My definition of strategy includes both; I use the terms corporate strategy and strategy interchangeably. Fundamental strategy defines the firm's basic concept and the concrete strategic decisions that make it up. The basic concept identifies the firm's goals; for example, when Daiei, the largest Japanese superstore chain, states that it aims to become a merchandising conglomerate, it is setting forth an image of its basic concept. Similarly, a food manufacturer projects its basic concept when it states that its goal is to become a diversified supplier of a full line of food products. A basic concept may not be concrete enough to establish specific policies. Still, it communicates simply and clearly the firm's basic direction and its primary mission.

The components of strategy are the product/market portfolio, the operations mission, and the resource portfolio (see Figure 1–1). The product/market portfolio includes the product areas and the markets in which the firm will operate and its strategy for doing so. A decision to diversify is a prime example of a product/market portfolio strategy decision.

The firm's operations mission decides what activities in the operations flow the firm will do internally. This component includes operations such as securing or producing parts and raw materials, as well as production and distribution to the final consumer. Even firms in the same product area handle these operations differently. One company

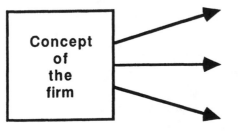

Products and markets
(what to sell, and to whom)

Operations mission
(what to do in-house)

Corporate resources
(what resources are required)

Figure 1–1. The components of strategy

may put most of its in-house effort into development of products, sub-contracting for most production steps and selling through an agent. Another may undertake the whole gamut of operations from obtaining raw materials to marketing.

The third element of strategy, the resource portfolio, requires decisions about what resources the firm will possess and what methods it will use to acquire them. Strategic decisions in this area will to a large extent determine the basic characteristics and capabilities of the organization.

In sum, product/market portfolio and operations mission decisions set the basic domain of the firm's activities: what to sell to whom and what operations to do in-house. The resource decision determines what capabilities the firm will have to perform those activities.

Quite often product/market portfolio strategy is given the place of utmost importance in the literature, with the operations mission and resource portfolio relegated to the background. Certainly product/market strategy is important, but operations mission and resource strategies are just as important, for reasons not always discussed explicitly. Each is an important ingredient of fundamental strategy.

After deciding which market to serve with what product, the firm still has a variety of choices regarding how to make and distribute the product to the customer. I will label the totality of operating activities *operations flow*. Others, including Porter (1980), have called it the "value chain." Operations flow includes research and development, procurement of raw materials, manufacturing of parts, assembly, distribution, aftersale service, and so on.

The firm need not perform all of these activities itself, but it must design the operations flow for its long-term advantage, independent of its product/market strategy. In selling the same product to the same market, one firm may obtain most of its parts outside, while another may produce them internally. Before 1970 many Japanese firms chose not to do their own distribution, concentrating their resources in production. Later, some began to take a more active role in distribution, realizing that doing so has benefits.

The firm must make two basic decisions regarding its operations mission. The most fundamental is: which operations should be done internally? The second is: how can the firm control the operations it has chosen to have done by others? I call the first decision *internalization* or *make or buy*, and the second decision *control*. An example of a control decision is: does the firm want to establish a long-term relationship with the parts suppliers, or will it deal with supplier firms at arm's length? Many Japanese manufacturers have chosen the first alternative with great success.

Both operations mission decisions have strategic importance to the firm because they often affect three factors at once: the amount of value added that accrues to the firm, the security and quality of the total operations flow, and the firm's long-term capabilities and adaptability. The first two factors often determine the firm's short-term competitive advantage, while the third relates to long-term survival.

By performing operations in-house, a company can internalize the value-added and the accompanying profit margin. This may make the product competitive in price or more profitable. This most visible economic benefit has been discussed explicitly in the literature.

A prime example of how the operations mission decision can affect the total operations flow occurred during the oil crisis in 1973. At that time the refineries owned by the major oil companies, which control their own crude oil supply, continued to operate steadily, while refineries dependent on other firms for crude oil were forced into a curtailed or irregular pattern of operations. Such instability was costly in terms of both manufacturing expense, because of irregular production scheduling, and customer confidence, because of uncertain deliveries.

Operations mission decisions affect the firm's long-term capabilities and adaptability because these decisions often determine the accumulation of invisible assets, as will be discussed in Chapter 2. In trying out some operational activity internally, the firm may learn a great deal about that process. This effect is not usually discussed, but it can be the most important one in the long run.

Take, for example, the Kao Soap Company's decision to strengthen its distribution network and market more of its products directly. Kao's record as Japan's largest and most profitable manufacturer of soap products is at least partially the result of this operations mission decision. Under its new distribution system, the firm continued to grow even after the oil shock raised materials prices substantially. That decision was described as follows:

> The secret of Kao Soap's success in soaps and detergents has been its rejection of the conventional wisdom on marketing channels in that industry. Creation of its own marketing subsidiary (Kao

Sales) and full use of that business operation has led to the current record of success. All the signs point to a strong company: ability to maintain adequate price for products, excellent marketing, research and development that turns out to be right on the mark, and low distribution costs. They have it all together. The roots of these success stories all go back to their system of direct marketing. Kao Sales has made Kao what it is today. (*Nikkei Business,* July 3, 1978)

Kao Sales, though it is a legally separate corporation, handles only Kao products and is really the marketing arm of the parent company. It now directly supplies more than 60 percent of Kao's products to pharmacies and other retail outlets. This internalization of distribution is the core of the firm's sales strategy. Begun in 1966, the Kao reform went against standard practice and thus had to endure a period of growing pains (it is not easy to drop existing wholesalers, for instance), but it has developed into a very successful operation. The four Kao company strengths stressed in the quote evolved from the tight connections between manufacturer and retailer. In this situation the manufacturer can more easily gather information on customer desires and market conditions and convince retailers to support its pricing strategies. All these invisible assets developed from the company's commitment to direct sales.

Had Kao maintained its indirect sales channels, it would have faced several problems. Wholesalers have their own ideas, which are often at odds with the strategies the manufacturer wants to pursue. Kao could not expect the same intensity of commitment it had for its own products, and information on competitors and customers would have been less timely and less complete. These problems with market information could have thwarted good production planning and product development. Indirect sales also may make it hard to carry out an effective pricing strategy. Maintaining good contact with customers and the market is the most important benefit of direct marketing. Kao obtained such invisible assets as a high-capacity route for acquiring information, accumulation of information on consumer desires, and influence over the distribution channels.

Internalization, of course, is not without costs. The firm must always be careful to balance the benefits against the two major costs:

increased investment and loss of flexibility. A substantial commitment of both financial and human resources is necessary to achieve the benefits of internalization. With its resources committed, the firm must incur fixed costs, and this commitment may not allow it to adjust quickly enough to changing conditions.

The Factors Surrounding Strategy

Of the factors surrounding strategy, the external environment is perhaps the most obvious. Unless corporate strategy follows the trends of the environment, a firm cannot continue on a path of high performance. The product/market strategy has to be in line with trends in customer demands, for example.

A strategy must fit with three factors in the external environment: customers, competition, and technology. Customer demands and competitors' behavior determine the basic character of the product market, and the trends and characteristics of the technological environment determine the firm's options regarding manufacturing processes as well as products. For each factor, I will discuss the conditions strategy must have in order to achieve environmental fit.

A firm's internal environment is made up of its corporate resources and the group psychology of the people in the organization. By utilizing these internal conditions effectively, the firm can implement its strategy and achieve the three elements of environmental fit. A successful strategy has to fit the resources of the firm and mobilize the employees. No firm's resources are unlimited, and each firm has a unique collection of them. The level of accumulated resources determines the range of strategies the firm can take. Moreover, in implementing strategy the firm may accumulate more and different resources. How does the firm utilize the existing resources, and how does it accumulate resources for the future? When strategy effectively solves these questions, it has achieved resource fit.

Strategy is implemented by everyone in an organization, from the chief executive officer to salespeople in the field and workers on the production line. The firm's performance is a result of many separate actions. A neat strategy document in corporate headquarters has no value unless it affects the actions of everyone in the organization. When a strategy mobilizes the psychological energy of the people in the organization, it has achieved organizational fit. An effective strategy gets people moving in a common direction.

The five kinds of fit that strategy has to achieve—three external and two internal—are shown in Figure 1–2. Each type of fit has a dynamic character; it must be maintained over time. Short-term static fit is not enough for the long-term success of the firm. The environment, corporate resources, and the firm's organizational psychology may change, either on their own or as a result of strategic intervention. Customer demand will vary over the life cycle of the product; new competitors may appear, and technological innovations will occur. Corporate resources are affected by strategy; the psychology of the organization can be inspired by an aggressive strategy or dampened by one that lacks inspiration. A strategist who understands that changes will occur need no longer formulate policy that simply reacts passively

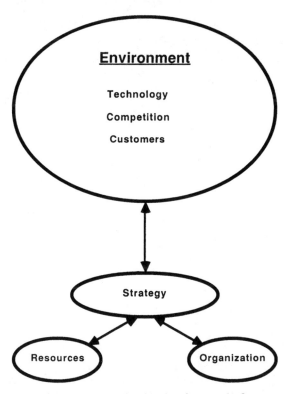

Figure 1–2. Five kinds of strategic fit

to external and internal factors. Because strategy can influence these factors, it can initiate and even create the changes it desires.

An important theme of this book is the relationship of strategic dynamics to static or short-term strategic fit. In some cases, a series of strategies in short-term strategic fit may happily lead to long-term strategic success. But in many other instances, strategic dynamics may be achievable only through a sequence that is imbalanced in the short term. Although this may seem inconsistent with the reader's idea of fit, static imbalance or lack of fit in some parts of strategy is quite often a prerequisite for overall dynamic strategic fit, leading to the long-term growth of the firm.

Levels of Strategic Fit

Strategic fit can occur at three levels: passive, active, and leveraged. Passive fit, the most conventional, takes the factors surrounding strategy as given, something to respond to, as in fulfilling existing consumer demands. But the firm can sometimes change the environment by a judicious choice of strategy or can at least anticipate external changes. Also, in the long run a strategy can certainly mold corporate resources and can, at least to some degree, mold the organization's psychology. In all these cases, the strategist needs to consider intervening in the factors surrounding strategy to steer them in a favorable direction. That is active fit. For example, the firm may try to persuade consumers that a new product, one they never dreamed of, is what they really want.

At the third level of leveraged fit, the firm does more than anticipate and respond to future changes in the environment; it uses those very environmental characteristics that are seen as limiting at the passive and active levels of strategic fit to make its strategy more effective. These factors make the firm's invisible assets more effective or permit the firm to undertake strategies using lower levels of invisible assets. In this sense, the effective use of environmental characteristics can be seen as leveraging a firm's strategy to achieve a higher level of fit. For example, there is currently a strong resistance to personal computers because it takes so long to learn to use them. Rather than see this environmental factor as limiting, a firm like Microsoft might put a major effort into developing a new type of operating system that addresses this problem. If the design is successful, the demand will spill over into other software products that the firm will sell and open up the opportunity to develop yet more products to fully utilize the resulting easier-to-use computers. Here the computer firm uses the seeming bottleneck of computer literacy to leverage its strategic efforts in software technology development.

Every firm tries to achieve passive fit, at least. But more firms fail, even at this level, than one might think. Active fit is less obvious and harder to attain, and fewer firms are successful at this level. At the third level, leveraged fit, only a handful of firms succeed. If one examines the strategies of firms renowned for continued strategic success, one finds that many are good at leveraged fit. They have a deep understanding of customer demands, competition, and technology. They know very well the characteristics of their resources and their people. And they know how to use all of these elements for leverage in their design of strategy. Each level of fit appears in the analysis of the five types of fit—customer, competition, technology, resource, and organization—in the following pages.

A New Strategic Logic

I would like to end this chapter by reviewing the logic of dynamic strategic fit and placing it in context. Three elements are especially important: the logic of invisible asset accumulation and utilization; the logic of dynamic, unbalanced growth; and the logic of human psychology, both within the firm and in dealings with customers and competitors. The first logic, of invisible asset accumulation and utilization, has already been introduced. In the second, the firm is concerned with its growth over time, which often requires a series of short-term imbalances in strategy. The third emphasizes human psychology. After all, it is people who make or break the strategy. The strategist must discover the logic that will influence people's psychology and capitalize on their strengths.

Conventionally, the logic of strategy has been predominantly that of economics: demand, market competition, capital investment, production, and so on. It has been mostly analytical. Yet the three logics mentioned above do not emerge from straightforward economic logic. All of them seem either alien to that viewpoint or erroneous. These logics are dynamic, soft, and behavioral. Of course, economic logic is necessary for strategy; it is a keystone. I do not want to downgrade its importance; rather, I want to upgrade the importance of the noneconomic, behavioral logic to its rightful level of equal recognition in strategy design.

Strategy has to guide the firm in dealing with the external environment, and here the primacy of economic logic is obvious. But strategy also has to lead an organization made up of people with various capabilities and psychological outlooks. This psychological component urges the strategist to emphasize noneconomic, behavioral logic. Obviously, both the psychological and the economic aspects are important. The holistic approach, integrating both types, is indispensable.

Invisible Assets

Chapter 2

Corporate resources are conventionally defined as the people, goods, and capital a firm can deploy to meet its short- and long-term goals. A small but increasing number of managers add information to the list. That final item is not easy to pin down. Technology is an example, but information is much more than that. Consumer trust, brand image, control of distribution, corporate culture, and management skill are all informational resources. I call these information-based resources *invisible assets,* and they are just as essential for effective operation as the more visible corporate resources. More than that, I believe they are the most important resources for long-term success.

Obviously all resources, visible and invisible, are necessary for a business, but two types of necessity must be distinguished here. Some resources, for example, the plant, must be physically present for business operations to take place; others are necessary for competitive success. Most physical, human, and monetary assets are necessary in the first sense. Most invisible assets and some human resources are necessary in the second sense.

An analogy to the resources necessary for painting a picture illustrates the differences between these two kinds of necessity. To make a painting, the artist has to be physically present in the room and has to have enough money to buy brushes, canvas, and paint. Human, physical, and monetary resources are needed to paint a picture, but not even these resources will make the painting a masterpiece. For that, something extra is needed, the painter's artistic sense and his technique—his invisible assets.

Importance of Invisible Assets

Invisible assets are the real source of competitive power and the key factor in corporate adaptability for three reasons: they are hard to accumulate, they are capable of simultaneous multiple uses, and they are both inputs and outputs of business activities.

AVAILABILITY AND FIXITY OF RESOURCES
Corporate resources can be classified in terms of how easy it is to change their level. The higher the cost of obtaining these resources from outside the firm, the more fixed their level is. The lower the cost, the more flexible those resources become.

Many invisible assets are quite fixed. There is no easy way to obtain a well-known brand name or advanced technical production skills in the market. Nor can money buy an instantaneous change in corporate culture or employee morale. Accumulation of these resources requires on-going, conscious, and time-consuming efforts; you cannot just go out and buy them off the shelf. For this reason, a firm can differentiate itself from its competitors through its invisible assets. If a resource can be bought, competitors with sufficient financial resources can gain access to it. And if a resource can be created quickly, competitors will have ready access to it through imitation. But competitors cannot do this easily with invisible assets.

Invisible assets have multiple uses. Take a firm's reputation with customers. Once established through successful marketing of a product, a good reputation can be used to promote another product. After Honda had built a reputation for quality in its cars and motorcycles, it was able to mount an ad campaign with the message, "Put a Second Honda in Your Garage" to sell its lawnmowers. Sophisticated technology also has multiple uses. Honda used its basic technology in small engines *sequentially*, first in motorcycles, then in cars, and later *simultaneously* in the United States in such varied products as generators and lawnmowers.

Only invisible assets can be simultaneously used in several areas. Obviously, a firm cannot use a worker in two different plants at the same time. And although an idle plant can be modified for a new use, the same floor space cannot be used for several activities simultaneously. Money put into one project cannot at the same time be utilized in other projects.

The important features of invisible assets—they are unattainable with money alone, are time-consuming to develop, are capable of multiple simultaneous use, and yield multiple, simultaneous benefits—make it crucial to carefully consider strategies for accumulating them.

Takao Ikawa, executive vice president of the Taio Paper Company, discussed how his firm developed such a strategy and prospered in an industry that has been in very bad straits since the oil crisis of 1973. "We have been working hard at modernizing what is visible as well as what is invisible. Plant and machinery can all be bought with borrowed money, but you can't buy invisible assets. Management means just one thing: creating invisible assets. We have spent a great deal of effort in constructing an organization, developing human resources, rules, and a cost accounting system, not to mention technology and brand name" (Nomura Management School, 1981). A firm's competitive power depends on the accumulation of invisible assets.

People are important assets of the firm, but they are important because much of the invisible assets of the firm are embodied in people; people carry and exchange the information necessary for strategic fit. I have emphasized the primacy of the information-based resources of the firm and its invisible assets, so at times it may seem as if I am relegating people to the background. I do not mean to contradict those who, like the Taio Paper executive, emphasize the importance of human resources. Rather, I want to stress that they are important because of their role in the development and maintenance of the firm's invisible assets.

Some invisible assets are embodied in people who do not work for the firm. Brand name, for instance, is held by customers, not employees. When we say that a firm has developed good channels to get up-to-date information about what its customers are thinking, it implies that the people who work at the stores which sell the firm's products hold a key invisible asset of the firm.

It is of course impossible to separate people from the invisible assets they carry. Engineers store technical knowledge in their brains; workers acquire skills and savvy on the job. These are examples of embodied information. People are important resources, not just as participants in the labor force, but as *accumulators and producers of invisible assets*.

INPUT AND OUTPUT RESOURCES

Invisible assets have another important characteristic that makes them valuable for strategy. While most corporate resources have to be used to achieve a successful corporate strategy, invisible assets can often be generated with no additional effort in the course of the everyday operation of the firm. Business operation requires inputs of people, materials, and money, but some of these resources are the outputs of the operation as well, and their dual nature makes them very important when designing a strategy.

Money is certainly such a resource, because it is a necessary input that comes out as cash flow. It can be recycled, with output from a previous project used as an input for future projects. Analysts have long understood that money is both an input and an output, but the dual nature of invisible assets has not been well recognized. Konosuke Matsushita, founder of Matsushita Electric, said, "Matsushita is a company that creates people." Not literally, of course, but people's capabilities are an important output of a business operation, as well as an input.

Information, similarly, is a dual resource. In the normal course of business, the firm acquires information not previously available, and this store of information can become the basis for the next project. For example, Epson started as a supplier of watch parts, then used its technological skills to become a major supplier of computer printers and other computer peripherals, including liquid crystal displays. This experience now permits Epson to consider expanding into such areas as miniature televisions (based on their liquid crystal display technology) and into office automation. Their president, Tsuneya Nakamura, stressed the dual nature of technology: "We are making a fresh and giant step forward in office automation. The hardware knowledge we have built up since our days of making parts for watches will be a plus for more systematic efforts in this growth field" (Nakamura, 1984).

Technological experience is not the only invisible asset that comes out of business operations, and the output is not always as conspicuous as in the Epson example. Chofu Engineering is a successful Japanese heating equipment manufacturer. The president, Yoneo Kawakami, summarized the dual nature of invisible assets very well. "If we can produce even one product which is better than those of our competitors, we can have business with retailers and establish a good business relationship with them. Once established, the relationship will make them willing to handle our other products as well. This opens up doors for us to enter the distribution channel" (*Nikkei Business,* Oct. 9, 1978). The Chofu manager is saying that in addition to improving earnings, having a good product has as an output a spillover effect of building a firm's reputation with retailers, thus affecting subsequent business operations positively. A company that has clearly superior products will develop information resources both in technology and in the distribution channel.

EFFECTS ON EXISTING ASSETS

Invisible assets created by business operations may have negative effects on the existing stock of invisible assets. Nikon's decision to widen its product line is a good example of the negative effect of a decision on an invisible asset, in this case, the Nikon brand name. Nikon, which had always been known as a manufacturer of cameras for sophisticated, professional users, decided in the late 1970s to broaden its product line and introduce a mass-produced single-lens reflex camera with many plastic parts for the less sophisticated user. That was a very fast-growing segment of the market and an area in which other Japanese camera manufacturers had been successfully expanding. The decision was not made easily. A Nikon retailer succinctly stated the worry of management: "There was serious concern despite the fact that this new camera would appeal to this new segment of young photographers. What would a long-time user of the top-of-the-line Nikon F think when he saw the less sophisticated EM model. Would the 'Nikon mystique,' so carefully cultivated over the years, lose its magic appeal?" (*Toyo Keizai Weekly*, July 7, 1979).

Indeed, the result was a deterioration in the overall strategy. Although some sales were made at the lower end, Nikon never succeeded in major penetration of that market segment. In the professional market segment, Nikon's reputation declined, opening the way for successful entry by the mass market producers. The Nikon example well illustrates the delicate nature of brand image, and how it can haunt the corporate strategist. Many other invisible assets, as we shall see, have potentially negative effects.

When an asset, be it money or invisible assets, is both an input and an output in business operations, it is important not just to consider its effective use as an input in current strategy, but also to recognize that more of that asset will be accumulated as an output of business operations. Strategy must take both input and output effects into consideration, as shown in Figure 2–1. Effective asset use as an input is sometimes incompatible with efficient accumulation as an output. If

the strategist is too concerned about using money effectively and for-
gets about efficient accumulation, then he may lose a great opportunity
to reap future large profits from an investment. Too much emphasis
on effective utilization prevents efficient accumulation.

This incompatibility is a problem with invisible assets as well. Nikon's introduction of the EM was an attempt to make good use of an
invisible asset, the "Nikon name." When the company worried about
jeopardizing its image with this new product, it was voicing concern
that using this asset would reduce its stock of invisible assets for future

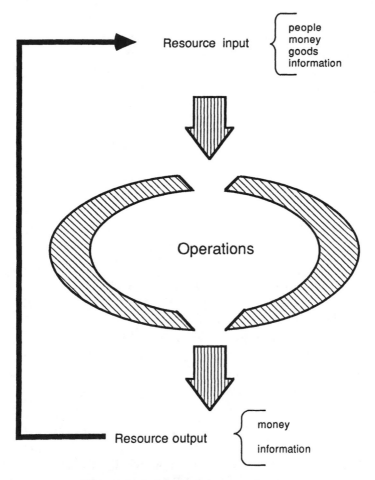

Figure 2–1. Resource input and output

use. This is not the only possible outcome, however. The EM could have triggered a break from Nikon's old image, which may be no longer appropriate to the current market. Thus one strategic decision the company must make involves choosing to use the brand image now or to maintain it for future use.

A Framework for Information Flow

To better understand the idea of invisible assets, it is important to recognize the close connection between those assets and the information, broadly defined, available to the firm. Abstractly speaking, information lies at the heart of invisible assets. By information-based invisible assets, I of course mean the stock of accumulated information in the firm, but I also include the channels that handle the flow of information of importance to the firm. In this definition there is a parallel to computers. Just as an information system in a computer has both data and the software to make that data useful to the computer user, a firm's information base has both information and the "corporate software" of information channels necessary to make effective use of the information.

From product development to production and marketing, each business operation has an associated flow of information. For example, those in charge of product development combine technological knowledge with information about consumer demand to develop new products. They do more than just combine existing pieces of information, however; they may import technological information from outside the firm (for example, through licensing), or generate new information in their labs. Information flow is everywhere in the product development stage.

In fact, information flows wherever decisions are made or human observation takes place. It is just as important in production and sales as in product development. Sales managers are always probing for trends in consumer demand, collecting information on consumer desires.

Information flow may be a by-product of the firm's daily activities. Customers may volunteer information on their preferences during normal negotiations, or a salesperson may be asked whether the company sells a related product. If the salesperson, without considering the company's possible responses, simply says, "We don't have it and I don't think we would ever consider making that kind of product," the salesperson may be transmitting to the customer the information that the company is unresponsive to customer requests.

Whenever one person is being observed by another, both actor and observer can learn something. The salesperson learns about consumer demands while selling, an engineer gains information in the course of product development. The information flow can go in the other direction as well. The person watching—perhaps a customer, colleague, or supervisor—also gains information about what the person is doing and about his performance. Not all information is important to the firm, but this perspective can provide important insights. For each information flow, there is an associated invisible asset.

Information can be classified as environmental, corporate, or internal.

Environmental information flows from the environment to the firm, creating invisible assets related to the environment. This type includes production skills, customer information, and channels for bringing in information. Note that both the amount of information and the capacity of the channels for obtaining that information are important invisible assets.

Environmental information can include flows from both the natural sciences and engineering to produce a key asset in technology. Even research and development can be seen as information gathering, the resultant flow adding to the invisible asset base of the firm. The stock of consumer information is created through learning activities in areas such as marketing.

Corporate information flows from the firm to the environment, creating invisible assets stored in the environment. This category includes such invisible assets as corporate reputation, brand image, corporate image, and influence over the distribution channel and its parts suppliers, as well as marketing know-how. This category also includes both the amount of accumulated information and the capacity of the channels that generate it. Brand name is an invisible asset created from the information consumers receive about the firm's products. Once the favorable information is accumulated by the firm's customers, that flow results in the invisible asset we call brand name. The firm's reputation is developed with its suppliers and the financial community in the same way. Both the stock of information in the hands of customers and suppliers and the channel's ability to transmit that information are important invisible assets.

Internal information originates and terminates within the firm, again affecting the invisible asset stock. This category includes corporate culture, morale of workers, and management capability, as well as the firm's ability to manage information, the employees' ability to transmit and use the information in decision making, and the employees' habits and norms of effort expended. Figure 2–2 illustrates the three types of information flow.

A high-capacity channel for handling the flow of information may be as important an invisible asset as the stock of information. For instance, a firm that has a well-functioning channel for bringing technology into the firm, such as cross-licensing agreements to exchange technology information with other firms, has an important invisible asset. Such a channel is valuable not only because it adds to the stock of information, but because it may also allow important decisions to be made without depleting that stock. The current situation in the deregulated airline industry in the United States gives a realistic example. Delta and United, which run on-line reservation systems, are able to

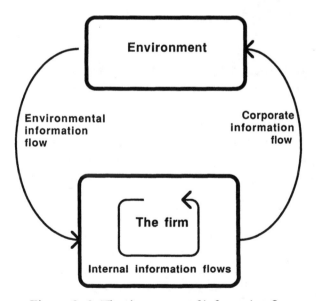

Figure 2–2. The three types of information flow

evaluate seat availability on an hourly basis and make decisions at least once a day on the number of discount seats to offer. Over a longer period this information allows them to decide on schedule changes in various markets. Information on seat availability must be used immediately to take advantage of changing conditions; the information is useless if stored, for tomorrow will be different (Conte, 1984). Many consumer product markets require similarly intensive information gathering. In the Kao Soap example, I showed that the direct sales channel was a powerful vehicle for gathering information about the environment.

Internal information also requires a channel. The information received from the environment and stored within the firm has to be directed to the appropriate decision makers quickly and accurately. Without an internal information flow system, the accumulated information does not have much value; it has to be used in strategic decisions.

Suppose the sales department finds out what kinds of products customers want. This information has to get to the people in charge of product development, who must then respond quickly. For this series of actions, the sales department must first obtain the information and transmit it to the product developers accurately. Second, the language used by the sales department and the product development departments must be mutually understandable. And third, the product development department must act quickly in deciding how to develop a new product. This flow of information is possible only when employees have high morale and a good corporate culture. That is not so easy to come by. Good internal information flow is a valuable invisible asset.

Market Share and Invisible Assets

It is sometimes said that a firm's share of the market is what determines its profitability. Studies by the Boston Consulting Group showed that costs fall with cumulative experience in production, but experience is also valuable because it generates informational assets. A large market share does not necessarily guarantee profitability, but there is a strong positive relationship between the two. High market share can lead to higher profit in part because fixed costs can be spread over a larger volume, reducing unit costs. Larger sales volume may also generate technological benefits; it may permit the use of mass production facilities, an effect that is often referred to as a scale effect. These factors are not the whole story, however.

A company with a large market share has at least two significant characteristics not shared by smaller firms. First, because business operations are on a larger scale, the firm has more cumulative experience in those operations. Second, the company has more contact with consumers through greater sales. These two advantages increase the firm's flow of information and thus increase the firm's invisible assets.

The first merit of large market share, the experience effect, will increase the firm's stock of information in production and sales. In a company whose business operates on a large scale over a period of years, the amassed environmental information can be quite substantial. This stock of information results in greater production know-how, better product design, and similar benefits. The firm also learns how to procure supplies and better understands critical points in sales. These benefits are reflected in lower costs per unit in production and sales. This is not the same as a mere mass-production effect.

The second advantage of large market share is the larger number of contacts with consumers, which results in more information flowing both to and from the firm. If many consumers have bought products with a given brand name, the brand is well known and the company can establish a good reputation. This information is the basis of invisible assets to the firm. At the same time, the company has more chances to pick up on consumer demand directly or as a by-product of contact, again acquiring valuable information. Salespeople should take advantage of the opportunity to gather information on customer demand. A firm with such a low-cost, highly efficient channel to collect information on consumer preferences will have an advantage. The information will help the firm to develop appropriate products, offer the right mix of services, and track the movements of competitors.

For example, Boeing gets information benefits from contacts with its commercial aircraft customers. Since it must maintain contacts with customers worldwide, it learns about problems that occur in the use of its planes (information it can use to make small modifications), and finds out what plans the airline companies have for the future. This enables Boeing to better forecast future demands in an industry in which there is only one chance in a decade to make major additions to the product line. A Japan Air Lines manager, whose company has the world's largest fleet of 747 planes, once said in jest that he should bill

Boeing for all the information JAL gives that firm on improving the jet.

Invisible assets due to large market share do not come automatically. A company must take advantage of the potential inherent in the larger market share to develop them. The indications the salesperson gets from the customers or the hints the technician picks up on the shop floor will do no good unless the firm's information flow system is designed to produce smooth communication and weed out irrelevant information.

Market share is not sufficient to create information-based assets, but it increases the chances that the firm will be successful in developing them. Large market share is not the only route to these benefits, nor is it a sure one. And even firms with small market share have the potential to create invisible assets if information flow can be activated.

Corporate Culture and Invisible Assets

"Corporate culture" is the phrase often used to describe an organization's chemistry. People label a firm as "sales driven," for instance, or say that a company has recently "become more bureaucratic." Corporate culture indicates the attitudes the organization takes as common sense and the types of thought processes and kinds of people it values. To define this concept in a way that is consistent with the information flow perspective, we can say that corporate culture gives each person in the firm a common and distinctive method for transmitting and processing information. It defines a common way of seeing things, sets the decision-making pattern, and establishes the value system.

For example, Hitachi Corporation's culture is said to have a strong orientation in heavy industrial equipment. This simply means that Hitachi has long been strong in this area and that this history has imbued its decision making and the actions of employees with ideas from that industry. Even in other product areas, problems are often approached from the industrial equipment point of view. The example also well illustrates how corporate culture is a product of and is accumulated through business operations.

The culture of the firm is an invisible structure that is powerful enough to shape the norms and rules employees follow. Their actions in turn determine the firm's performance. Sales and profits are the results of actions by many people. In a sense, each bit of work an indi-

vidual does is a starting point for determining the company's performance. If the work is not done well, performance suffers.

Whenever employees take actions, they are making decisions and
processing information. Among the key factors that influence these
decisions are the policies handed down by management. Performance
and behavior evaluation techniques also play a part in that process of
communication from top management. Equally important, however,
are workers' understandings of the tasks they are supposed to do, the
permissible approaches to those tasks, and the expected levels of effort.
These norms both direct behavior and put restrictions on it. In fact,
they are the corporate culture itself, which has the power to control
and direct each bit of work in the organization.

Masatoshi Itoh, the president of Itoh Yokado, a prominent chain of
Japanese superstores, which are a combination of department store
and supermarket, emphasizes this point:

> Once you get everyone in the company to think that the customer
> is what we are here for, you can be sure that the customer will
> always be in people's minds, whatever happens. In your own
> house, you don't always have to tell people what to do. There is a
> climate that develops that gets things done. We strive to get that
> same climate working in our company. Step by step, we build this
> climate that values our customers and suppliers, and I think this
> ultimately determines the outcome in our business. Sure we
> haven't got it rock solid yet, but I really consider this one of our
> strongest assets. I always tell that to the new people we hire every
> year when I meet them formally on the first of April. I tell them
> it is their responsibility to take care of that asset. These intangibles
> are much more important than we ever realize. Success in retail-
> ing doesn't come from showy maneuvers, but requires constant,
> steady accumulation of seemingly insignificant efforts. (Itoh,
> 1980)

Accumulating Invisible Assets

TWO ROUTES

Invisible assets are accumulated in two ways. In the direct route, a firm
takes explicit actions to achieve that goal. Good examples of the direct

route are television commercials that try to create a brand image, research and development conducted by a project team to develop a particular technology, and training programs to teach employees that the customer always comes first. That approach requires little further explanation.

The discussion here will focus instead on the second route, the operations route, in which assets are accumulated as by-products of daily operations. In that sense, this route is indirect. Examples of the operations route are also easy to find. If a product is well designed, a firm can develop a good reputation without further effort. For example, manufacturers of very high quality audio equipment depend on word of mouth to spread their reputation. When there was a downturn in the Japanese economy in the mid-1970s, Mazda sent many of its engineering and production staff out to car dealerships to try to increase sales. When these people returned to their jobs after the crisis had passed, they had an increased appreciation for the importance of customers' demands. Here again, the invisible asset of a "customer first" orientation was enhanced in the course of the company's operations.

Choice of product line can sometimes be a factor in accumulating invisible assets related to manufacturing. Honda's experience in motorcycle production in the United States made it easier to enter the American automobile market and operate its American automobile manufacturing plant later.

Matsushita's overseas experience also illustrates this point. When the company opens a plant overseas, it often begins with the production of dry cell batteries. The company then progresses to other electric products (fans, radios, televisions), depending on the local market demand. This pattern is the result of a conscious strategy. Arataroh Takahashi described the company policy as follows: "In every country, batteries are a necessity, so they sell well. As long as we can bring a few advanced automated pieces of equipment for the processes vital to final product quality, even unskilled labor can produce good products. As they work on this rather simple product, the workers get trained, and this increased skill level then permits us to gradually expand production to items with increasingly higher technology levels, first radios, then televisions" (Takahashi, 1980).

The activities of the firm may produce several invisible assets simultaneously. Timken, the large American manufacturer of bearings, is a good example. One of Timken's competitive advantages is strong customer service and technological support provided by well-trained sales engineers. *Business Week* (May 17, 1982) quotes the following comments by three of Timken's customers: "When a part fails, a customer does not have to return it. Instead, Timken engineers inspect the problem on site to determine its precise nature and help the customer get his equipment functioning." "A Timken sales engineer helps us to design the bearings in our gearbox." "Timken engineers check the assembly process every two weeks. They are scrambling in our behalf." Why do Timken's engineers spend so much time in the customers' plants? Certainly providing better service will give the company a competitive edge; the engineers are there to outperform the competitors in service. But the heavy emphasis on service also helps Timken accumulate the three types of invisible assets: environmental information, corporate information, and internal information.

First, because it is heavily involved in the customers' operations, Timken can collect a substantial amount of information about their desires (and perhaps learn about future trends in those desires). The firm can see how their bearings perform and see what went wrong, perhaps, with a particular model. In terms of both the information stock and information flow, Timken's direct service system is beneficial. Second, by frequent contact with the customers' engineers, Timken can supply information about its products, inexpensively influencing the customer's purchase decisions in Timken's favor (corporate information). Third, constant contact with customers' requests, complaints, and pressure helps maintain a customer-oriented culture at Timken (internal information).

As I emphasized with market share, these invisible assets are not created automatically. Sales service must be effectively managed with an explicit understanding that one of the aims is to accumulate invisible assets. Without that aim the costs of maintaining an extensive sales engineering team cannot be justified. Timken's service force is an excellent example of the operations route to invisible asset accumulation.

I cannot stress too much that the operations route is an attractive and efficient alternative to the direct route. To have an effective operations route, management should keep two key points in mind: first, have a clear picture of the effect of daily operations on the stock of the firm's invisible assets, and second, keep in mind that on a day-to-day, down-to-earth basis the implementation strategy has great effect on invisible asset accumulation. This has many significant implications. A firm whose long-term performance has declined without any apparent reason or one that has been just barely hanging on may not be accumulating adequate invisible assets by the operations route.

When a firm fails to accumulate additional invisible assets, it loses in two ways. Not only does its pool of assets fail to increase, but the basic structure of its invisible assets can be weakened as well. The failure of the process often has an additional negative effect on the firm.

Accumulation of invisible assets through the operations route may take longer than through the direct route, but it is often more reliable and steadier. This difference is apparent when we compare the brand image created by a television commercial with one created by word of mouth. The television ad has less credibility than an acquaintance who has used the product. A potential consumer who needs more information can follow up with the person who recommended the product. This is not to say that a firm should never use the direct route. It is often possible, and may even be necessary, to use both routes together. A strategist who understands the advantages and disadvantages of the two routes can arrive at the best mix.

CONTROLLING INFORMATION FLOW

Successful accumulation of invisible assets comes down to control of the information flow. If a company wants to accumulate technological know-how, it is best to have key stages of manufacturing done in-house and keep the information proprietary. Many computer manufacturers try to develop semiconductors and large-scale integrated circuit chips (LSIs) themselves. Letting others do it may give away too much information.

Casio, the Japanese electronics company, provides a good example of how keeping key stages of production in-house can help a firm accumulate technical know-how. One of the largest manufacturers of digital watches and calculators, with significant market shares in electronic cash registers and musical instruments as well, Casio was only a small manufacturer of relay calculators in the 1960s. One key element in the company's success is its unique approach to the control of information flow. Casio saw the LSI semiconductor chip as the basis of its competitive position in many product areas. Although it does not produce the semiconductor chips itself, it keeps tight control over the design steps in bringing an LSI to production.

Before an LSI sees the light of day, it must pass through three design stages: deciding which functions the chip should have, transforming these functions into a series of logic circuits, and blueprinting the layout of the electronic circuits on silicon. Casio chose to concentrate its resources on the first two stages. Although most calculator manufacturers stop at the functional design stage, Casio carried its design responsibility one step further. Creation of the circuit layouts is closely tied to production facilities, so Casio, which does not manufacture its own LSI chips, does not control the last stage.

There are several merits to having the logic design done in-house. New designs can be developed quickly, and the designs can be original. Relying on standard chips would not enable unique design. If chip manufacturers did logic design, Casio would have no assurance they would do it in a timely manner. But the most important advantage is the accumulation of skill in LSI chip applications.

The turning point in Casio's LSI chip design strategy came about 1970 when the calculator battle heated up and standardized LSI chips came into wide use in the United States. The three manufacturers that eventually emerged to dominate this industry (Casio and Sharp in Japan, Texas Instruments in the United States) did not follow the move to standardization, but insisted on developing custom LSI chips that set their products apart. Of the three, only Casio chose not to manufacture the LSI chips itself. A Casio research and development manager, Noriaki Shimura, had this to say about the company strategy:

> When most manufacturers chose standardized LSI chips, the handwriting was on the wall: the outcome of the electronic calculator war was in effect decided. The three winners all believed in the importance of LSI chip design. This belief led them to develop products with strong market appeal. At that time, custom LSI chips sold at a premium, and we took a lot of heat within the organization for our decision. Some people saw it as a waste of money. The Casio semiconductor engineers that worked on these custom chips turned out to be invaluable resources for our company. They are responsible for our many innovative products that set Casio apart from our competitors. (Shimura, 1979)

Casio's LSI chip and digital technologies, which were developed and nurtured through desk calculator technology, have been adopted to watches and electronic musical instruments to expand the product line. Even though Casio did not make watches at all in 1973, by 1979 it had become a leading manufacturer of digital watches. Its success stems from its strategy of extending its internal operations to the key stage of LSI logic circuit design, where it was able to reap the benefits of expanded know-how. Casio's decision shows that the operations mission decision is much more complicated than a simple "make or buy."

In marketing as well, the decision about how to structure the distribution channel is more complicated than whether the company should own its own distribution network. A company that wants quick access to market information must often own part of the distribution network. Kao Soap did this by controlling direct sales. It may not be necessary, however, to own the distribution network to gain control of information. Close contact with dealers who have a strong commitment to the product line, a commitment the firm can nurture, may be just as effective in achieving control over this important information base. It may not be necessary, however, to have complete ownership of the process to gain control of important information flows. A firm may be able to utilize the know-how of other companies by jointly working to develop these invisible assets.

The firm must answer two questions concerning the control of information. One is how to identify the critical activities that will carry the most important information. The other is how to control these critical activities and the flow of information. This problem is illustrated in Figure 2–3.

An example will clarify how a strategist answers the first question. Suppose the company wants to evaluate alternative operations that will provide information on customer demand. Selling directly to retailers is one alternative, or the firm may be able to gather information through its handling of claims and customer service. A third option would be to expand into retailing and have daily contacts with customers. The strategist has to decide which of these three operations will be the best source of information.

Once the firm makes that decision, the second question, how to control the flow of information, becomes important. Two related decisions must be made: first, *who* will perform the critical activities; and second, *what mechanism* will ensure that the information actually flows as intended, both in quality and speed. If the firm decides to have outside people observe buyer behavior, for example, it must decide who will do it and how the information will be transmitted—through distributors, say, or by the firm's own sales force. Internalizing a critical activity is normally the best way to assure initial proprietary access to information. That is why some firms prefer direct distribution systems, as the Timken example showed. And many firms manufacture key components for their final product internally; IBM, for example, produces its own memory chips. Firms do this partly because they cannot afford to allow others access to sensitive information on key components and partly because the technological skill they acquire will help them develop a competitive final product.

Obviously internalization is not always the best decision, even if it looks good from an information control perspective. Some activities may require too much fixed investment to internalize and may be too risky. Partial internalization, say 25 percent of components made in-house, may be sufficient. In that case it becomes imperative to arrange a mechanism for keeping some control of the information.

REPERCUSSION EFFECTS

All decisions about strategy have some repercussions for invisible assets. If a firm wants to develop a new product, it has to accumulate the required invisible assets. The new activity associated with the new

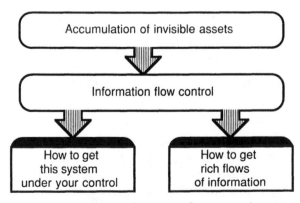

Figure 2–3. Information flow control

product will then generate yet more invisible assets. Alternatively, if the firm launches a project that everyone derisively labels the president's pet project, the corporate culture will be affected negatively and employee morale will be lowered. This is another type of repercussion on invisible assets.

As I pointed out earlier, implementation strategy also affects the firm's invisible assets because it determines how the firm's daily operations are carried out. If management decides to create a specialized assembly line, for example, the product development people may be encouraged to develop further products that can be produced on that assembly line. They may be tempted to do this even if the product does not fit the market completely. Implementation is usually thought of as short-term strategy, but when we consider its effect on invisible assets we can see that it is significant for long-term strategy as well. The Matsushita strategy is a good example of this, since its emphasis on battery production creates invisible assets for more ambitious strategies later on. Any long-term strategy must pay attention to the repercussion effects of implementation strategy.

An ideal strategy creates a dynamic cycle of corporate growth that is centered on invisible assets. A firm's current invisible assets limit the effective range of its product/market portfolio and operations mission. Implementation of the current strategy will create a new set of invisible assets, superseding the old set. This process in a sense renews the firm, which can then undertake new ventures. In this view, corporate growth becomes almost synonymous with the growth of invisible assets.

Corporate strategy is the organization's blueprint, and all of the elements of that strategy must be closely interrelated. Product/market portfolio, business operations, corporate resources, and implementation strategies all must mesh. Of these, corporate resources, especially invisible assets, are the most important; they serve as the focal point of strategy development and growth.

Customer Fit

If a firm is to grow and prosper, its strategies must fit the external environment as well as the firm's internal resources and its organizational characteristics. Environmental fit, the most complex and perhaps the most important of the three types, is made up of customer fit (discussed in this chapter), competitive fit (discussed in Chapter 4), and technological fit (discussed in Chapter 5). Although I discuss them separately, these three elements are not really independent of one another. A firm must consider environmental fit as a whole if its strategy is to be successful.

The Bundle of Customer Desires

Matching customer desires seems simple enough. The firm continuously provides products the customers desire and good, reliable service. Of course, no company sets out to ignore customer desires or provide inadequate service, but ironically, the strategies of many firms work against their own interests in this area. Matching customer desires is a complicated, difficult task, and it is central to effective strategy.

Developing a strategy to match customer desires requires knowing who the customers are, yet many companies neglect this first step. A firm obviously knows who its existing customers are and can easily generate a profile of them. This, however, is not enough; the firm must identify the target market and determine what that group of customers wants.

The consumer wants a product to satisfy a bundle of desires. He wants not just a single service, but a bundle of services. Take automobiles, whose basic function is transportation, of course. But in purchasing a car, a consumer looks for many other characteristics as well;

different sizes, design options (for example, air conditioners), and colors project different images to the world and satisfy different desires. Service facilities, delivery time, and financing terms may also be important items in the bundle. Clearly, a successful auto company like GM or Toyota does not sell just vehicles themselves, but a bundle of services.

This point is so important that I will give two more examples. The first, Hakubi Kimono School, shows that this principle applies to services as well as products. Ostensibly the school teaches young Japanese women how to put on a kimono, a skill many postwar women in metropolitan areas did not learn as they were growing up. But in fact the school satisfies several desires. An executive of the company stressed the bundle of characteristics they offer: "You'd think all we do is teach how to put on a kimono, but there's more to it than that. Our students also see our school as a place to socialize. We emphasize the social function of the school, marketing it as a place where students can share interests and build friendships" (*Nikkei Business,* July 16, 1979). Because Hakubi understood that its students wanted both instructional and social services, it has garnered a 70 percent share of its market. For both services and products, the story is the same. A firm that identifies the characteristics consumers want and provides that bundle will be successful.

These principles also apply to sales of mainframe computer equipment. Under the slogan "IBM Means Service," that company has built and maintained a dominant position in that market. It has sold not just the products, but also the services customers want. Of course, customers pay for these services indirectly by buying the product, but they feel that the services are worth it. IBM also sells its software with the promise of good follow-up service. Once again, a bundle of services is provided.

Consumer desires can be classified in three categories: product functions, supplementary services, and price. It may seem that customers are concerned only with functions such as the quality and design of the product, but supplementary services and price are often just as important. The supplementary services category includes service after the sale, payment terms, convenience of purchase and delivery, and product image. At the same level of product characteristics and supplementary services, consumers prefer a lower product price.

The bundle of customer desires will change over time because of changes in attitudes and because of the products introduced by competitors. To adapt to these changes, the firm must change the elements in the bundle of services it offers; it must still continue to balance the three types of consumer desires. If a firm has a really high-quality product, but the price is not right, buyers will not flock to the door. Apple found this out the hard way with its Lisa personal computer, yet it seems to be succeeding with a lower-quality, much less expensive variation, the Macintosh.

A product that is weak in one element may be able to make up for that if the other elements are especially strong. A product that is a bit high-priced and not quite up to par in performance may still sell well if the supplementary services are especially attractive, if the product is easily available, credit terms are easy, and delivery is fast.

Many firms have used supplementary services to find distinctive markets for their products. Takara Belmont, a Japanese manufacturer of chairs for beauty shops and barbershops, illustrates the point that a small firm can use supplementary services to satisfy the bundle of customers' desires. For Takara, ease of purchase became the key strategic characteristic. The firm's chief executive officer described the strategy: "Except for some chains, most barber salons are small scale, too small to make a major capital investment. To help them, we hooked up with banks across the country. We developed our own financing system, calling it the 'Takara Barber/Beauty Salon Loan.' With the payment now extended over a period of three to five years, the shops were able to replace their old chairs with our product" (Industrial Bank of Japan, 1979). Takara did not stop there. It provided management advice on store design, construction, and merchandising for new shop owners and even helped plan the opening ceremonies. Management advice extended to providing technical seminars and assistance in training beauty shop employees.

Precisely identifying customer desires is no easy task; there are many pitfalls along the way. These pitfalls include: incorrectly identifying the firm's customers, having preconceived images of customers' desires, and confusing customer desires with "noise" in the information channel.

The firm has to gather information about its real customers. If it does not identify those customers correctly, it cannot possibly achieve customer fit. In a less extreme case, the firm is not paying sufficient attention to a key group of customers. A restaurant chain might assume that parents are the key customers when a family goes out to eat. After all, they pay the bill. Yet it is almost always the children who decide where the family will eat; the parents probably are indifferent. A restaurant that pitches its advertisements to parents will be wide of the mark because it is not correctly identifying its real customers, the children. For a firm selling parts to a large corporation, the real customer is often the head of the purchasing department. Unless they identify that person's desires and values, the salespeople will get nowhere.

In defining the customer base, the firm has to be aware that the final user of the product may not be the person who makes the purchasing decision. Here strategy has to take both parties into consideration. Aluminum windows are a good example. The final users, the family that will live in the house, rarely decides which manufacturer's windows to buy; that decision is the contractor's. So the firm should think twice about whose desires it wants to satisfy, the family's or the contractor's, and where to make its appeal. For the family, waterproofing, soundproofing, insulation design, and color selection may be important; the contractor will want windows that are easy to install and have few problems after installation. Timing of delivery to meet his construction schedule may be crucial. A product has to meet the demands of both of these buyers if it expects to succeed in this two-tiered market.

The second pitfall is holding preconceived ideas about customers' desires. Although some firms have already decided what their customers want before they begin to investigate customer desires, many companies think they are being objective when they investigate their customer preferences. They set out, hoping to find that the customers agree with their own ideas for the product (a perfectly natural wish), and this makes it likely that their investigation will reach the conclusion they want. Since this tendency exists even in the most well-meaning investigation of customer preferences, every firm has to watch carefully that it does not fall into this trap.

The question for the strategist is, "What do our customers want?" However, the unwary strategist may instead ask a different question, "What would we prefer our customers' desires to be?" The first Kentucky Fried Chicken store in Japan was out in the suburbs, easily accessible by car. That was the kind of store the foreign firm knew how to design, and it would have been convenient if Japanese consumers had found that pattern attractive. However, in Japan nearness to train stations is more important than accessibility by car, and Kentucky Fried Chicken had to adjust to that preference before it could succeed in the Japanese market. What can a manager do to avoid this pitfall? He must put himself in the place of his customers. If Kentucky Fried Chicken had taken the time to find out how Japanese commute, instead of imposing an American notion, it would have succeeded more quickly.

The third pitfall is failing to take into account distortion in the information channel. A firm can sometimes forget that there is always noise in the channels it uses to gather information on customer preferences. Not everything it hears about customer preferences is important or even correct. The second pitfall involved interpretation of people's desires; this one concerns the problems that arise as the information is picked up and transferred to the strategist.

Noise can come from customers themselves. They may not purposely present a false image of their desires, but when a customer says, "These are the characteristics I want in your product," a firm should not assume that the preferences expressed represent current or even latent desires. The customers may not have thought the problem through well enough to be aware of all their desires, much less to be able to concisely communicate them.

Many companies study customer complaints to learn about their clients' real preferences. If carefully analyzed, this information can tell a lot. When people are angry enough to submit a claim, they generally have thought through the problem and communicate it clearly to make sure that the firm will take action. As a result very little noise is introduced.

Another type of unintentional distortion occurs when third parties gather information. If a firm contracts with an outside agency for market research, the answers to preference questions may not reflect the customers' true desires. The strategist has to use a noise reduction system to decode market research results so that they can be used in making strategy decisions. A manager cannot do a good job of decoding the information if she never leaves her desk at headquarters. To do this effectively, she should gather some information firsthand by having personal contact with customers. Alternatively, a manager can find another information channel, such as complaints information, that is likely to have less noise. Careful attention to service after the sale can often help the strategist identify changes in the bundle of consumer desires before they become obvious to competitors. A manager can find information about consumer desires at every point of contact with customers.

Strategies for Customer Fit

Consumer desires have three qualities that a strategist must recognize: bundles of desires are not uniform across customers, they are not stable over time, and interaction among the elements within the bundle is important, as Figure 3–1 shows.

Even within a single market, a firm cannot expect every consumer will have the same bundle of desires. There are always several groups each with smaller differences across individuals, that have varied preferences; some are most concerned with price; others are more interested in quality. A firm that considers all of Japan as a homogeneous

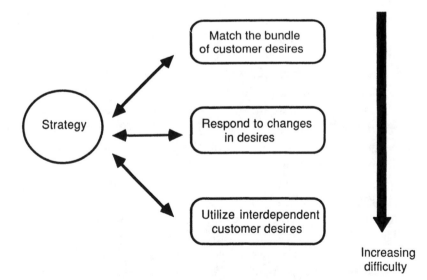

Figure 3–1. Three levels of customer fit

market might decide that thirty-five-year-old male white collar workers in both Tokyo and Osaka have similar preferences in clothes. But consumers in the two cities are quite different. The Osaka "no nonsense" consumer lives in the commercial center of Japan, while the Tokyo consumer, in the nation's capital, has more aristocratic tastes. The same styles of clothing will not sell equally well in the two cities.

Defining a product line or market as homogeneous can lead a strategist astray. Phrases like "a line of prefab homes" or "the automobile market" give a false impression. Customers for luxury sports cars are clearly different from those who purchase economical compacts. Even within the compact car market, single people and families want different types of vehicles. Singles want good design and a powerful engine in a compact car, while the families put more emphasis on interior comfort and room. Most markets are made up of varied segments that emphasize different elements in the bundle of consumer desires.

Even in a product as seemingly simple as instant coffee, firms cannot assume that a single kind is sufficient for all markets. Nestlé, a Swiss company, has been very successful in Japan because it has marketed instant coffee with its worldwide brand name Nescafé, but using a blend especially tailored to the Japanese taste. Said a Nestlé dealer in Japan, "It may be the same Nestlé brand name, but an American customer probably wouldn't drink the beverage the Japanese customer delights in" (*Japan Economic Journal*, Mar. 1, 1983).

A similar lack of uniformity exists in industrial goods markets. Both small and large companies use machine tools, but their demands are different. The small firm does not have the trained staff to repair complex machines, and if a machine is down for a day, the firm may incur a substantial loss. This customer will trade sophisticated functions for reliability and quick service response. Good credit terms may also be important. In a large firm, multiple-function machines and lower prices may be the primary requirements. Since consumer desires are far from uniform, the firm has to decide how to satisfy each segment of the market, deciding, for example, whether it has the corporate resources to supply that segment at a reasonable cost.

The strategist must keep in mind that the consumer's bundle of desires changes over time. No consumer will always have the same elements in his bundle, nor will each element have the same importance over time. The reasons for changes in the bundle of desires are quite diverse. Incomes rise or fall; technology progresses; people's living patterns change; the age distribution of the population changes. Company strategies and market patterns may also influence consumer desires. Demand for a product may change over its life cycle; new competitive conditions in the market may alter what the consumer wants. A firm may foster subliminal preferences or change the intensity of existing preferences. For example, people did not know they wanted a pocket calculator until companies called their attention to the desires this product could satisfy. The firm should look upon changes in consumer desires as opportunities for further growth. Adapting to changing customer preferences may be the most important aspect of long-term customer fit.

The third essential point to understand about consumer preferences is that the elements in the bundle influence each other. This kind of interaction occurs within each consumer's preference bundle, as well as between consumers. A change in one element of a person's bundle of desires will affect the other elements, and may affect the desires of other consumers as well. A good example is the manager who buys a personal computer for home use. If she gets hooked on it, she will be more favorably disposed toward buying office equipment with computer capabilities. The emphasis placed on individual elements in the bundle may change as well. Having driven an economy car for a while, a person may decide he wants a little more comfort and choose a more deluxe model next.

Thus firms should consider carefully how their products will change the buyer's preferences and be prepared to satisfy the future bundle of desires as well as the present bundle. This means not simply providing extensions of the present choice, such as accessories for a car, but providing the next stage in the development of the consumer's preferences. That next stage is often a logical result of the current purchase, as the examples above show. When a home is built with wiring for a sophisticated cable system, the provider of the housing must satisfy a whole new set of demands: the homeowner will want electronic equipment and perhaps instructions for using the system.

Changes in a customer's bundle of preferences can influence the preferences of other consumers as well. If a company that has introduced robots on its production line improves its efficiency, other firms will follow their lead and look for a whole new set of characteristics in industrial machines. The manager who loves her personal computer may convince the people who work with her that they want one at home too. In cross-customer relationships, people's desires are likely to be interdependent. Some interdependencies occur naturally; some have to be created by the firm. By understanding the relationships among elements in each customer's bundle and between the preferences of different consumers, the firm can more efficiently fit its strategy to the customer. This interdependence in the customer's bundle of desires enables the firm to use that bundle as a lever to increase demand for its products. Using that lever can make it easier to gain access to customers for other products.

When Casio used its semiconductor chip and liquid crystal display technology for low-cost word processors and pocket televisions, it was able to build on the good reputation it had developed with its watches to sell other products. If people had not gotten used to consumer products such as watches that use semiconductor technology and liquid crystal displays, they would have been less likely to accept the small, portable word processors and miniature televisions that use that same set of technology at a more sophisticated level. An approach that uses the interactions of consumer desires is probably more efficient than dealing with each of the elements separately.

Corresponding to the three elements of customer desires, there are three levels at which a firm must fit its strategy to customer desires. From level one to level three, the degree of difficulty increases. To achieve customer fit, the strategy must first match the bundle of customer desires (level one), then adapt to changes as customer preferences develop (level two), and finally find ways to capitalize on interactions among those desires (level three).

Matching the Bundle of Customer Desires

How can firms use the bundle characteristic to respond to customer desires? Three points are key: decide which element in the bundle to focus on, pay close attention to the bundle as a whole, and clear away bottlenecks that keep customer demands from surfacing.

First, the firm must clarify what part of the customer's bundle of desires it will focus on. There are never enough resources to be the most appealing on every characteristic in the bundle; if for no other reason, the product will no longer be attractive in price. It is not sufficient to have all the elements in the product, service, and price areas be average, nor does it make sense to make each characteristic better than that of competitors by the same amount. A strategist must decide which will be the selling points; something must make your product stand out from the competition. Each of these elements requires an expenditure of corporate resources, and these scarce invisible assets of the firm have to be concentrated.

The strategy has to be adjusted to the marketing focus. If product quality is the selling point, then corporate resources must be heavily weighted toward development, design, and quality control, and the corporate culture must be strongly oriented toward technology. If supplementary services are the focus, strong marketing, a good service distribution system, and adequate financial resources are required. If low price is to be the core of the appeal, cost reduction becomes a must; resources will be concentrated on continuous investment, rationalization of the production operation, production skill, and efficiency of the material supply system.

It is obvious that the selection of a marketing focus cannot be divorced from decisions about the operations mission, that is, which parts of the operation should be done within the firm. Once a marketing focus is chosen, the elements of the operations mission that will create the firm's advantage in the focused area must be kept under control. A firm like Sony, which emphasizes the quality and advanced functions of its products, cannot leave development to others. To produce an innovative color television, Sony developed its own one-gun system for projecting the picture onto the screen; it could not just buy what was available in the market. Sanyo, which competes to a greater extent on price, bought the technology it needed to produce color televisions at lower cost. Sanyo cannot, however, purchase or contract for manufacturing technology in the market. Low cost is its marketing focus; it must develop that capability in-house to maintain its competitive position. Note that both Sony's and Sanyo's market focuses have led to competitive success in the color television market. If a firm wants to focus on supplementary services, those services must be kept under tight control, perhaps with all of the work done in-house.

A firm cannot let others do the essential functions of its marketing focus and expect to remain competitive. One Japanese firm had always chosen to make product characteristics its marketing focus. On one product, however, it was under great pressure to get its costs down and, to do so, contracted out parts production. It did this not just for standardized parts, but even for the parts that were the core of its product's competitive position. In effect, its product development became controlled by outsiders, and the company lost the key to its marketing strategy, the ability to develop new products.

In choosing a focus, each firm must consider its own corporate resources. Thus it is not surprising that firms with different focuses succeed in the same industry. A comparison of the post–oil-shock strategies of the two top firms in the prefab home market in Japan—Misawa Homes and Sekisui House—will drive this point home. While Misawa has focused on product function, Sekisui has concentrated on supplemental services. Misawa concentrated on innovation; its "O-type house," introduced in 1977, had excellent acceptance in the market because of its modern design, larger size than competing models, standard luxury features, and attractive price. A later model used a ceramic building material for the first time. Misawa continued to introduce refinements to its product line, and its research labs looked for further innovation to attract customers (Misawa, 1984).

Contrast this with the Sekisui approach based on supplemental services. The buyer can custom-order much of a Sekisui house, and the company has built a good reputation for follow-up after the sale. In contrast to Misawa's use of sales agents, Sekisui sells directly to customers in order to provide thorough supplementary services, the core of its marketing focus (Nagata, 1979).

But a firm must not focus on one element so intensely that it ignores the other elements in the consumer's bundle completely. Misawa does not ignore supplementary services; Sekisui does do product development. Each desire in the bundle must be met to some minimum degree, or the product will not attract customers. The entire bundle of consumer desires has to be in balance, as shown in Figure 3–2, even as it maintains a marketing focus as a core. There are many examples of products that failed because they lacked that balance. If price is set so far below the competition's that the company has no money to spend on developing brand image and providing supplemental services, the result will be failure.

A single element is often the key to the emergence of demand for a product. Price is often a barrier. Many new products penetrate the market more rapidly after sales reach about 20 percent of the customer population. At that point, production costs start to decline rapidly, so the price can be lowered. The cost of supplying supplemental services also goes down at that threshold level. It then is worthwhile to provide such services to attract customers who see service problems as a barrier to buying a product. For example, a person might resist buying a camcorder because he is afraid that it will require service. Once the service system is in place, however, he can depend on it not just for repairs but perhaps also for advice on using the camcorder.

Identifying and removing the barrier can be a very effective way to create new consumer desires. The specific element that creates the barrier will change with the environment and the size of the customer base, but the potential strategic gain will always be there for the firm to exploit. Sekisui House has always watched for and taken advantage of each new barrier in consumer demand. This is one reason it has continued to have high growth even when the economy has been sluggish and other firms in the industry have suffered. The company explained its strategy as follows:

> Until 1975, access to financing was the bottleneck in selling new homes, but since that time, land availability has also become a serious problem. Therefore we have begun to supply land and housing as a package to the customer. We buy up a plot of land a developer has gotten ready for us, and sell the individual lots to

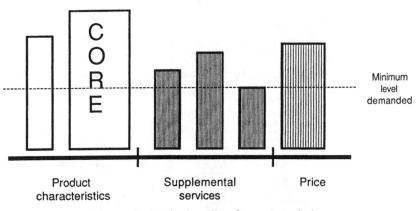

Figure 3–2. The bundle of customer desires

our customers along with the housing we manufacture . . . Last year (1978) a survey showed that half of the homeowners wanted to trade up and move to better homes. They often had trouble selling their old homes, since there was not a well-developed resale market. Without such a resale market, sales of our new homes would be dampened. Thus, in the spring of 1977, we established Sekisui Real Estate. (Nagata, 1979)

At each opportunity, Sekisui concentrated on a single characteristic that was restricting purchases. Timing was important. If the company had tried to develop the housing resale market in the early 1970s, when it was not easy to get financing for purchasing a larger home, the strategy would have been off the mark, yet it was one key to a successful strategy in the more mature market of the late 1970s. The same situation—changing barriers and changing requirements for corporate strategies—exists in other maturing industries, such as the automobile industry.

SEGMENTING THE MARKET

Not everyone wants the same characteristics in a product. There is no "average customer." In almost every market different customers want different characteristics or different levels of the same characteristics. Demand may also grow faster among some groups of consumers than others. A single strategy, trying to match all these segments uniformly, is likely to fail.

Three rules to follow for effective market segmentation are: first, find a unique way to segment the market; second, narrow the focus to one or a few target groups; and third, minimize the problems that arise from segmentation. The first problem a firm faces in segmenting the market is to find a unique criterion, which is not necessarily the most convenient one. Finding a unique criterion achieves two goals simultaneously: it determines the firm's focus on the bundle of consumer desires, and it provides the necessary guidance for developing specific segmentation policies.

No one classification of customers—or even a combination of classifications—will lead to the unique segmentation. Firms have used a wide range of classification schemes successfully: customer demographics (age, sex, educational level, income, occupation), geographical divisions, product characteristics (price range, intended use), and such characteristics as psychographics (economy, convenience, and status of the product). The strategist has to carefully consider the particular customer and market conditions in making this choice.

The firm must then choose among the many potential segments that the classification scheme provides. Here too the strategy must have a focus and not try to appeal to every potential segment. Only when the firm concentrates its resources and appeals to one or a very few segments can it expect to be competitive.

A Japanese clothing manufacturer, Renown, was a late entrant to the men's clothing market. Its first move was to segment the market by age and focus on a particular age group. The brand it initiated, Durban, was an immediate success, and the Durban company is now an independent firm with a major share of the market. A book on the company's management style described its strategy:

> Two companies, Van Jacket and Jun, clearly had each targeted segments of the young market. Two other large firms were oriented toward older men, but did not seem to be focusing on any particular segment. Durban saw an opportunity to target one segment of this older market. Durban chose as its first target the thirty-five-year-old, college-educated white-collar male working in one of the large metropolitan areas. At that time, men in their early thirties were not the largest group in the population—the twenty- to twenty-five-year-old group was the largest. Renown figured, looking ahead ten years, that if it could establish itself in that market segment now, the firm would then be ready for the growth potential as this twenty- to twenty-five-year-old group matured. By looking ahead, Renown developed a successful strategy. (Yamasaki, 1978)

Some might criticize Durban for focusing on such a narrowly defined segment; even if the company succeeded in capturing that segment, the market might be too small to make the strategy a real winner. Durban believed it was chasing more than just this narrow current market, however. If it succeeded in that one market, its reputation would make it easier to pursue other customers later. In my opinion, this wider view of the segmentation goal was the key to Durban's strategic success. The company followed the pattern shown in Figure 3–3.

Durban did choose a specific age-group target, but of course they sold to other segments with similar tastes. Middle-aged men in smaller towns who like to think of themselves as cosmopolitan and well-dressed might buy the same suits. So might a young man who wanted to feel that he had arrived in the business world. These repercussion effects can be important. Once the suits sold well to the original target market, the company had established a clear brand image and a good reputation. But without the success in the initial target market, that would not have been possible. A firm needs to focus first if it wants to have wider market acceptance later. Invisible assets like reputation lie behind these repercussion effects.

The firm should also take care to avoid the negative consequences of oversegmentation. While concentrating on a few segments, it must be on the alert for weak points that result from segmentation. Breaking down the market into more and more finely differentiated segments does not always pay off. As the market is divided more finely, the company may try to satisfy the desires of many small segments, resulting in smaller, less efficient production runs. With so many group desires to juggle, the production and marketing system may become increas-

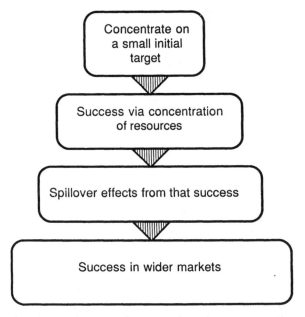

Figure 3–3. Stages of successful market segmentation

ingly costly to manage. With so many segments to watch, it is easy to miss a change in the bundle of consumer desires in one segment. Failure to respond to the change may jeopardize the firm's competitive position. Tight management control may be able to avoid these difficulties, or the firm may choose to compete only in closely related segments. The benefits of market segmentation directly conflict with the benefits of large-scale production.

There are several ways around this problem, however. Since most economies of scale are in production, the firm can concentrate its segmentation in marketing and supplementary services. A software firm could sell to sophisticated users through mail order and provide more services to another segment. Another alternative is to find similar segments in overseas markets so that the firm can achieve the gains from economies of scale. This may be the strategy of many smaller Japanese businesses that depend on foreign markets.

Another alternative is to find ways to produce products cheaply in the volumes necessary for the chosen level of segmentation, perhaps through automated design and production. Standardizing production processes (for example, for interchangeable parts of automobiles intended for different markets) may be possible. Or a firm can develop a family of products from a single basic design to maintain some production economies.

RETAINING CURRENT CUSTOMERS

Retaining customers requires some specific strategies. A customer who commits to dealing continuously with a firm has become, in effect, the firm's invisible asset. If the firm lets the customer get away, it has lost that asset and must go through the effort of reacquiring a valuable resource.

It takes less effort to keep existing customers than to attract new ones. If the customer switches, she must gather new information and establish a new trading relationship with another company, a process that is costly for the customer. But that switching cost is an asset for the firm that wants to keep its existing customers. There are many examples of switching costs. If a customer's plant is designed around the machinery supplied by a particular firm, the customer faces the costs of a complete redesign if he switches suppliers. And workers, used to the current production system, must be retrained. These costs can mount up quickly. In both personal and mainframe computers, software is often machine-specific. Once a firm's data are entered on one system, it incurs reprogramming costs as well as the chances of unreliable operation if it decides to switch machines. Here time costs are added to the money costs of switching.

A regular customer expects salespeople to show up regularly without being called. The salespeople know the firm and its products well as a result of these frequent contacts. If he switches to another firm, the customer has to wait until the new salespeople reach the same level of understanding of his operations; initially he must put more effort into the sales relationship.

When a customer purchases a firm's product, she is making a hidden investment. As the transactions continue and the firm provides on-going service, an information base is built up. This is a kind of investment for the customer; it is not an explicit part of the deal between the firm and the customer, but it comes along with the deal. Customers, consciously or unconsciously, make an investment in the business relationship. As the customer invests in the relationship, the firm accumulates invisible assets related to that trading relationship. A customer's good relationship with a stockbroker, for instance, is an invisible asset for that firm. When an office buys a "smart" typewriter, the workers get used to the benefits of office automation, and that office may then buy more sophisticated office automation equipment from the same company. The workers' acceptance of office automation is an invisible asset for the supplier firm.

A firm can raise the costs of switching by inducing the customer to increase that investment and by raising the value of the investment, so that the customer willingly accepts higher switching costs. Examples of the first approach are easy to find. The firm can design products specifically for key parts of the client's operations. Or it can make its products an integral part of the customer's design process, thus increasing the customer's investment. Computer manufacturers accomplish this by sending service engineers and programmers to help a customer install the system.

If the firm provides good after-sales service, and salespeople make calls at appropriate times, the customer will respond by giving more information, again increasing his investment in the relationship. The strategist who says, "Marketing really begins after the sale," is emphasizing this aspect of customer fit.

The second point, increasing the customer's valuation of the investment, is clearly illustrated by IBM's decision on the software for its personal computer. Instead of continuing its policy of developing most software in-house, early in the hardware development process IBM published sufficient information so that other companies could have a wide variety of software ready when the PC came out. With a large software base already in place, the person who ordered the PC felt the investment had really high value; as a result, the IBM PC became the standard for that generation of personal computers, and IBM developed a loyal customer base. Its customers, willingly hooked on the IBM system, are unlikely to switch brands. If a firm can make its product the industry standard, customers will find it hard to switch.

Adapting to Changes in Customer Desires

The second level of customer fit requires adjusting to changes in customer desires. Dealing with change requires both a different time frame and a different emphasis. If changes in demand are predictable, the firm's response can be more specific; for example, information channels can be created to monitor the changes, and the firm's product portfolio can be adjusted in advance. Major changes that are hard to forecast require a different emphasis. Rather than adjusting the product portfolio, the firm must make a change in its accumulation of strategic resources.

To match the changing bundle of customer desires, a strategist must prepare plans for forecasting and satisfying those changes, organize a system that responds to these changes quickly, and accumulate invisible assets for responding to changes that cannot be forecast. This may seem straightforward, but all three steps have to be done simultaneously, and this is harder than it looks.

When changes are predictable, it is possible to prepare a strategic scenario that takes them into account. One way is by actually initiating a change through new technology, products, or customer service systems. To illustrate the value of precipitating changes in consumer desires, consider the bold strategy Casio took in 1974 when it realized that demand for watches would move toward digital watches. It cut the price of its digital watches to half of the usual price at that time. The forward-looking strategy was described as follows:

> When Casio decided to enter the market, there was not much demand for the digital watches. Casio could enter at the current price level and nibble at the existing market demand, or cut its price in half and try to take a big chunk out of that larger market. The way Casio figured, by cutting the price to cost at full capacity, demand would increase rapidly as the word got out to consumers. For a time, until consumers adjusted, losses would be inevitable, but it would, Casio thought, be worth it. As it turned out, Casio's strategy was right on the mark.
>
> As the market developed, Casio started to try to do creative destruction in its own product line. In just the last half year, Casio has introduced more than one hundred twenty new models into the watch market. Casio seems to be willing to intentionally destroy an existing market in which it is participating, while simultaneously creating the market that will replace it. (Nagata and Tokunaga, 1979)

Casio's low prices created additional sales, and frequent additions to and changes in the product line turned out to be an excellent way to monitor evolving demand. This strategy can be extremely effective when a new product is widening its appeal. At that stage neither the company nor the consumer knows the specific demands to be satisfied, though they may have some vague ideas. The company probes for the mother lode of new demand through experimentation. When the demands are known, there is a plan to tap them.

Whatever the source of an anticipated change, a firm has to be prepared to take strategic advantage of the new bundle of desires. A firm that makes the first move to identify or change demand has to have the resources for the next stage ready to take advantage of its earlier move. It cannot use all the arrows in its corporate quiver to achieve the initial objective.

For example, it has been relatively easy to identify changes in food shopping patterns as more women work outside the home. More shopping is done in the evenings and on weekends. To match this change, food retailers can be open for longer hours or, as Japanese grocery chains have done, have some smaller stores that are open late for this segment of the market. A person's first car is often a small economy model. Since a rise in income is rather easy to forecast, the automobile company is prepared with more luxurious or sporty models for the next car purchase. Having a full product line enables the company both to respond to changes and to push consumers toward a new product.

These strategies share one characteristic: a product or service is ready to take advantage of an expected change. This means expanding the product portfolio in anticipation of the change. The customers, of course, must be able to distinguish between the various products in the portfolio—they must see a Buick as different from a Chevy—or the products will cannibalize each other. If the products are too far apart (as seemed to be the case when Apple added the sophisticated Lisa to its workhorse Apple II line), people will not be able to move easily from one to another. If the gap between products is too great, competitors may seize the opportunity to occupy that niche, creating a barrier for customers moving between different products in the firm's line. Few Apple II owners had sufficient funds for or interest in the sophistication offered by Lisa, and Apple lost customers who wanted to upgrade until it came out with the less sophisticated but cheaper Macintosh.

Meeting changes in consumer desires often involves making drastic adjustments to the existing product line. Simply adding a product may not do the job. If consumer desires are changing rapidly and overall demand is falling, the appropriate strategy may be to begin a strategic withdrawal from this market. Of course the firm should keep some products there, but not its main resources. Such a strategic withdrawal necessitates reallocating resources to develop other areas of the product portfolio. Long before it actually enters the new area, the firm has to accumulate the necessary invisible assets.

A well-planned withdrawal can pay off handsomely, as Honda's experience shows. Honda was strong in minicars in the Japanese domestic market in the late 1960s, but it realized that these small vehicles would not succeed in the international market. It chose to reassign the resources from minicars to subcompact cars:

Honda reasoned that such small, underpowered vehicles did not have international appeal and were near the end of their product cycle, but that larger autos still could expect a period of significant growth on world markets. Fortunately, Honda had profits from its motorcycle business for seed money. In the early 1970s, Honda prepared for an orderly retreat from minicar production, and readied its first subcompact automobile product, the Civic. It introduced the Civic in 1972. Just two years later, in 1974, while it still had the largest share in the minicar market, it withdrew from that market. (Mito, 1977)

Honda was able to assess the future of a product that was still very profitable. The withdrawal worked brilliantly and pushed Honda to become a world-class competitor in automobiles. If they had continued with minicars, the result might have been very different.

SENSING CHANGES

To profit from changes in consumer desires, the firm has to learn about them earlier than its competitors. If the information system is operating well, it may identify these demands even before consumers articulate them. To be useful for strategy decisions, an information system must be able to quickly and accurately sense changes in consumer desires, and it must be able to communicate the changes to the right people. To satisfy these two conditions for meeting the ever-changing mix of consumer desires, the firm must develop a structure that keeps a close eye on customers and has a tight and solid channel for transmitting information from customers to people in the firm.

Kinhisa Mushakoji, managing director of the largest Japanese glass firm, Asahi Glass, set up such a system by assigning a research and development section to each operating division. He said, "New ideas for products should start from the market, where you can keep in constant touch with the customer." The purpose of the reorganization was to assure that the information would not only be gathered, but would also be communicated quickly to the key people—the product development group.

An organization's ability to sense changes can be improved in several ways. Senior management can create a corporate culture that emphasizes watching for changes, an environment in which "the customer is king." A firm can also use market segmentation to make changes in consumer desires more visible. Market segmentation focuses attention and makes it easier to track the dynamic marketplace. But if the organization is asked to gather information on a market that is too diffuse, important changes may be overlooked. Another way to anticipate change is through market experimentation. Products that test the limits of consumer acceptance can serve as antennae for shifts in desires. Casio's introduction of many new digital watch models provided this kind of information.

The communication channels from the customer to the firm are like telephone lines. If the connection is not good, the listener will not receive the information, even if he knows its source. The communication system may include direct sales channels, which monitor consumer preferences directly. The importance of direct sales cannot be overstressed, but it is not the only way to communicate. A firm can develop products jointly with its customers, or the engineers can help with sales activities so that they know what consumers want and understand the language of the marketplace. Claims for after-sales service can be monitored. All these methods for communicating information require direct contact and open exchange with customers, thus adding to the firm's invisible asset base.

A good example of information gathering is the system American Express set up when it decided to offer its Gold Card in the Japanese market in 1980. American Express understood the importance of staying in touch with the rapid changes in the consumer credit market, which was just beginning in Japan at that time. The firm installed computer facilities to monitor all transactions and get a picture of the patterns of card use. After analyzing the data, the firm was able to pinpoint its advertising to particular groups. Along with the computer system, American Express used two-person teams of foreign and Japanese employees to monitor commercial card users (Lehner, 1982).

CORE INVISIBLE ASSETS
Some changes are very uncertain or impossible to predict. The further into the future one looks, the less likely it is that even a trained marketing strategist can forecast the changes. To deal with uncertainty, management must build up resources that can be commited when unexpected changes occur. When Honda moved from manufacturing

motorcycles to building minicars in 1960, they accumulated technology and marketing resources that allowed them to enter the subcompact car market in the 1970s.

A firm needs to have a *core* resource, which it can accumulate in sufficient depth so that it is a useful basis for responding to unforeseen changes in consumer desires. The core resource will be different for each firm; it may be in such diverse areas as technology (a light-weight alloy for planes), customer service (an entire system designed to use a robot), or production (a low-cost assembly line to make many kinds of calculators). Not all such resources are equally valuable. The firm should choose the one with the greatest potential for dealing with uncertainty. The firm's strategic response to changes is set once the core invisible asset is decided on. If a firm's effort is spread too thin, if there is no focus, the response to changing consumer desires will be ambiguous.

By concentrating its efforts to accumulate invisible assets on a core area, the firm will be more likely to learn how to cope with uncertainty. Without a deep pool of core resources to draw on, the firm will not have sufficient strength to respond to unexpected changes. The Kyowa Hakko company, founded in 1947, had as its initial core resource fermentation technology, using microorganisms for the production of alcohol. Because of the depth of accumulation of that technology over time, the company was able to draw on that deep pool in other areas as well. As it applied this technology in the manufacture of wine and of various kinds of chemicals, it further increased the sophistication of its already world-class core technology. This expertise permitted the firm to expand into areas such as biotechnology, a field no one could have predicted when the firm was founded.

At times a firm may have to change or add to the core of resources. Earlier I stated that new products can best be developed when a basic product is doing well and can provide support. The same is true for resource accumulation. The time to search out and develop a new core resource is when the current core is working well. When that resource loses power, it may be too late to develop a replacement. Honda developed its auto technology while its motorcycle technology was still strong.

One thing that can be done at any time to make it easier to match unknown changes is to create a corporate culture rich in entrepreneurial spirit and prepared to challenge the unknown. It is the people in the organization, after all, who will have to deal with the changes in customer desires; strategy succeeds or fails through their actions. An organization that does not value change may not take advantage of promising new technology. Conversely, an organization used to dealing with change may get through some difficult times as it tries to find, by trial and error, the appropriate response to changes. This kind of corporate culture can be the most effective tool for adapting to changing customer desires.

To build such a culture the strategist can see to it that the company always has a very visible new area of business. This makes employees sensitive to new things and creates a value system based on participation in new developments. In a new venture unit, there is tension and conflict, plenty of room for trial and error, but people's spirits are high, and they enjoy the challenge. The rest of the organization can sense that atmosphere, and a positive attitude is implanted.

Second, the physical environment where people work day to day will influence the corporate culture. The workers' tolerance of change will be influenced by the type of machines they work with and by the material they handle. People's ways of thinking change to fit what they work with. If a firm installs machines that require a rigid regimen, workers may be worried about the chaos that will result from a change. If a firm creates an inflexible operation, it will not have the adventurous spirit it needs to adapt to change.

For a long time banks had to deal only with fixed-rate products, so they were never able to develop the "change is good" mentality. In this era of financial revolution, this corporate culture is a hindrance to full exploitation of new opportunities. Securities firms, on the other hand, have always dealt with risk and change because the prices of securities are subject to daily fluctuations. That corporate culture has prepared them for the more turbulent financial markets of today.

Decisions about a firm's portfolio of technologies and even about the plant and equipment will thus influence the attitudes of employees. Managers have to consider these effects and be careful not to create an environment in which thinking patterns become too conservative. One leading Japanese machine tool manufacturer fell into this trap. During the 1960s, one of its products was a big hit. The company was on all the lists of excellent companies and was very profitable. It installed specialized production lines to meet the fast-growing demand for the product. Most of its invisible assets were related to that product, which dominated the market.

In the early 1970s the firm was hit from two sides. Demand for the product fell, and competing firms developed good substitutes. The company, slow to respond to these changes, ended up losing money and firing many employees. One reason for the slow response was the specialized production equipment, which, without their realizing it, made people conservative. The company worked on developing only products that could use that valuable equipment. They associated good times with the successful product and held on to outdated design concepts. Here past glory trapped a firm and kept it from changing. This kind of thinking may have kept Volkswagen from changing its classic beetle model, and U.S. auto firms from investing in assembly lines to produce subcompact cars. In both cases, investments in specialized assembly lines helped determine the corporate culture.

Using Customer Interactions

At the third level of customer fit, the firm capitalizes on two types of interactions of customer desires: interactions between consumers and interactions within each customer's bundle of desires. Customers have contact with each other, and this first type of interaction has potential for use by the strategist. In addition, I will emphasize the contribution a combination of customers can make to a successful overall strategy.

The ability of existing customers to attract additional clients may be the easiest interaction effect to grasp. If a well-known company adopts a firm's machining center, other companies will follow their lead. Trend-setters exist in every market; if a firm can attract them, they will attract a wider customer base over time. Attracting trend-setting customers also establishes a firm's credibility and brand image and generates word-of-mouth advertising. These invisible assets can be deployed as the market develops. Since trend-setters have such a high potential value, it pays to spend resources and energy to attract them. The strategist must of course have a plan for using the spillover effects to attract the wider customer base. Again, unless the strategist has these additional arrows in his strategic quiver, his efforts will merely make money for his competitors.

Attracting trend-setters also has a demonstration effect, as customers are seen using the product. Passersby notice that a restaurant is crowded each night, and they may stop to try it themselves. People crowded around a bargain table at a department store draw yet more people to the area. If a person buys a new car, his neighbor feels that his car looks a little older. This demonstration effect has helped launch many consumer goods and even industrial products. Consumers become walking advertisements for a firm. Remember how people turned to look at the first owners of the Sony Walkman. The visibility of the product allowed Sony to attract many customers at no cost. A company can use aggressive techniques to attract a customer base large enough to create a demonstration effect. Some firms use low introductory prices to boost initial sales; others advertise to create an image for a new product. Some products are designed to attract attention when people use them; for example, the first hand-held electronic games made unusual sounds.

Interactions among the desires of a single customer can also be used to achieve customer fit. If a firm buys a robot to do welding, it may then consider buying a more sophisticated robot to do materials handling. A customer may go to a securities firm simply to buy a money market fund, but if that turns out satisfactorily, she may buy some stock later on. If a homeowner is satisfied with the contractor who builds his house, he may hire him later to add a room. Buying a new dress or suit often leads to purchase of new shoes and other clothing. In all these cases, satisfying one desire leads to another desire.

Consumer desires tend to cluster; as one is satisfied, a related one comes to the surface. To achieve this interaction effect, the firm should take actions that make customers likely to buy more than one related product, and it should create a system to satisfy the cluster of desires it has stimulated. Sears Roebuck developed just such a strategy. Sears recognized that the cluster of customer desires related to some of its major product lines, for example, home and car equipment, included services as well as goods. Sears acted aggressively to make its stores one-stop centers: it bought an insurance company, a securities firm, and a real estate company. As a result, it can provide very close substitutes for the services provided by banks. It also expanded its services for coordinating home remodeling. A customer can buy, insure, and maintain a house through Sears. Housing finance is provided by the mortgage arm of its real estate firm. When a home is sold, the proceeds can go into a money market fund or other securities offered by the Sears brokerage firm. Insurance can be bought at the insurance counter, and new appliances around the corner. Remodeling and repairs, including design, installation, and materials, are handled in the next section. Customers attracted by this cluster of housing services and products then feed back to other parts of the store as well.

THE MIX OF CONTRIBUTIONS

The strategist can capitalize on yet another customer interaction by choosing a balanced mix of customer contributions. Usually, solid customer relationships can make various contributions to the firm, as shown in Figure 3–4. These contributions can be categorized as contributions to current sales and profits, to sales and profit growth, and to invisible asset accumulation. Even within a single category, different customers may make different contributions. In the first category, con-

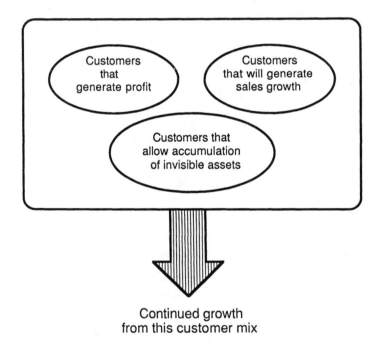

Figure 3–4. A mix of customer contributions

tribution to current sales and profits, one customer may contribute to the current period of high profit through small volume; another may generate a low profit margin, but guarantee large and dependable sales volume. Another may fill the seasonal gaps in production. Similar differences can occur in customer contributions to sales growth and future profitability. The contributions of invisible asset accumulation may also occur in various ways. A demanding customer will push a firm's technical staff to solve his problems, increasing the staff's experience and level of expertise. Trend-setters or prestigious customers can help establish brand name, another invisible asset.

A company should strive for the right mix of customers to achieve each of these contributions. The more a strategist can mix the three classes of contributions—profits, growth, and accumulation of invisible assets—the better the effect. It pays to include at least a few customers who are not able to contribute much now but have a bright future. A strategist may even choose to do business with a customer that will never be a major source of profit but that can teach the firm some useful technical or market lessons.

A Japanese electronics parts company turned itself around by effectively using a mix of customer contributions. Though the company's performance had been lackluster, its engineers were able to develop an outstanding product and take the largest share in that market; more important, it has held its ground. Three types of customer contributions made up the necessary mix. First, the firm supplied the main part for an innovative company. That customer pressed for cost reductions and was oriented toward marketing. It encouraged the parts firm's product development, pushed up sales, and taught the importance of careful design and marketing.

The second type of customer was a group of smaller, overseas mass production plants that generated a stable, reliable sales volume throughout the product development period. This volume generated sufficient profit to allow the firm to undertake product development. The third type was a prestigious foreign firm that taught the parts manufacturer some important lessons in high technology. Doing business with this firm also gave the parts manufacturer the seal of approval for its product.

There were of course other reasons for the company's success, but the contributions of these three customer types were crucial. Behind the international successes of many Japanese firms one can find similar stories: with the right mix of demanding domestic customers and stable-volume customers, the firm can obtain both profits and the invisible assets necessary for international expansion. Although a single customer may be able to contribute more than one element to the mix, such a customer is hard to find. A strategist can create an optimal mix by finding the customers that will make the appropriate contributions.

Competitive Fit

The essence of competition is the creation of a difference between the firm and its opponents. Competitive fit requires creating and exploiting a competitive edge. A firm can create that competitive edge in various ways: by choosing different market segments from its opponents, by making a cost-reducing investment in a large-scale plant so it can compete in the same segment, or by controlling distribution channels, for example. Behind these are two basic categories of competitive behaviors: confronting competitors directly (attaining and maintaining advantage) or developing ways to avoid competition, to win without fighting. The second way is less costly, but it is more difficult to achieve.

To achieve competitive fit, a strategist can, first, use the firm's competitive edge to win out over competitors (competitive advantage); second, create strategies that are hard to counterattack (secure strategies); and, third, create strategies that cause competitors to withdraw (winning without fighting). As the firm advances on these three levels, the effectiveness of its strategy increases. Of course, each level is increasingly difficult to achieve. The three levels of competitive fit correspond to three different notions about the nature of the competition, as illustrated in Figure 4–1.

The goal of the first level is to be different from competitors, perhaps through a cost-reduction strategy or through product differentiation. There are many choices at this level.

One's competitors, are not duplicates of one's own company; they have their own characteristics even if they are in the same industry, have the same level of technological sophistication, and target the same market segments. A firm can use that difference to create a competitive advantage. The strategist can make customers differentiate between the firm and its opponents if he has a detailed understanding of these competitors, as well as of his own firm's advantages. The first level of competitive fit is thus based on differences between the firm and its opponents.

The second level focuses on the potential response by competitors and tries to make counterattack difficult. It is important to understand the combative nature of competitors: they will not stand still as a firm develops its own competitive advantage. Their ability to strike back will of course be restricted by the conditions they face, but it is best to assume that all competitors will respond in spite of barriers. If opponents can easily counter a competitive position, that strategy will have little lasting benefit. If the firm lowers prices without lowering production costs, for instance, competitors can strike back quickly. It is a much better strategy to force competitors to take time and effort to counterattack.

A firm that succeeds at the second level may be able to get to the third level, where competitors cease to be opponents. Exceptionally good strategy at the first two levels can form the basis for winning without fighting, with its lower competition costs. As long as a potential competitor stays out of a firm's markets, it need not be labeled an opponent. This is true as well of a firm that decides to cooperate. Examples of cooperation between firms are the Toyota–General Motors plant in California and the Amdahl-Fujitsu tie-up on mainframe computers.

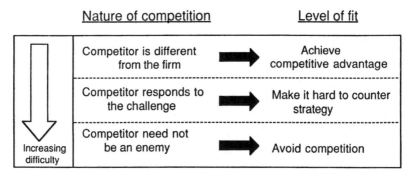

Figure 4–1. Three levels of competitive fit

Identifying the Competitors

At any level of competitive fit, it is necessary to first identify the competitors. Strategy will succeed or fail depending on whether the firm correctly identifies its opponent. The key opponent in one market may be a minor factor in other markets with different conditions. Coca Cola does not have to consider Dr. Pepper as an important competitor in most American markets, but in the south, Dr. Pepper is the major competitor, and Coca Cola must adjust its strategy accordingly. Firms must also anticipate potential competitors that may appear as environmental conditions change. Who in the Japanese restaurant industry would have dreamed that Japanese palates, used to noodles for lunch, could be won over to a Big Mac or Kentucky Fried Chicken?

Obviously, companies that sell the same products are part of the competition to be identified, but just as important may be firms that seem peripheral. The managers of IBM's Selectric typewriter division could easily spot competing electric typewriter firms, but should IBM consider portable electric typewriters as competition, or manual typewriters? What about printing services? For a customer who wants an attractive mailer or a series of form letters, a printing service may be a good substitute for IBM's products. Identifying the direct competitors and even those on the periphery is not enough, as IBM found out to its dismay. For years, most of IBM's competitors were other manufacturers of electric typewriters, initially from Europe, but with some later entrants from Japan.

But when a new set of competitors came into the market with innovative technology from the semiconductor industry, they had a major impact on IBM's position. Electronic typewriters and, later, word processors changed the shape of competition in this market. As computer printers have improved the quality of their output, at speeds much faster than an electric typewriter, word processors have replaced typewriters. This has changed the market for both typewriters and copying services. IBM has had to face three types of competitors: producers of the same kind of typewriters, producers of direct substitutes, such as word processors, and producers of other services, such as desktop publishing services, that satisfy the same bundle of consumer desires.

As I have stressed, market conditions as well as competitors are not static, but evolving. It is necessary to watch both existing and potential competitors. Even as strong a firm as IBM can be temporarily knocked off its feet if it does not anticipate the evolving nature of its competition.

As a product moves through its life cycle, the competition may change. When IBM introduced electric typewriters, it had only manual office typewriters to worry about. As the market developed, producers of electric typewriters were the main competitors. Then related industries challenged the norms and posed a competitive threat. IBM had to change its strategy as the cycle progressed. The strategy it used against electric typewriter manufacturers could not effectively counter the new features and functions offered by smart typewriter manufacturers and word processing companies in recent years.

Another reason for identifying the competition is that doing so allows the firm to use market segmentation to narrow the field of competitors. A firm can often choose its competitors. In the IBM case, Selectric typewriters were targeted for business offices and high-income households. With this strategy, IBM did not have to compete with the firms that sold portable electric and manual typewriters to middle-income customers for home use. For a long time IBM was able to control the competitive environment in its selected market, where its product lines and corporate resources were superior to those of other firms in this segment. IBM's market segmentation strategy was successful.

Creating a Competitive Edge

In creating a competitive edge, the first level of competitive fit, the strategist must decide what weapons to choose, how best to use them, and how to efficiently develop these weapons. The struggle between firms for customers takes place at various venues. Sometimes the fight is over price; at other times, it is over new product development or supplementary services. Each firm has to decide what area it will fight in; in so doing, it chooses its weapons. The marketplace may dictate which weapons are to be used, but frequently, the firm can choose, and that choice will often determine the outcome.

CHOICE OF COMPETITIVE WEAPONS

Since all participants are scrambling to satisfy consumer desires, the ones with the strongest weapons will win out. The competitive weapons chosen indicate the elements of the bundle that are being appealed to. Competitive weapons can be classified as those based on product characteristics (product differentiation), those based on supplementary services (service differentation), and those based on price differences (price differentiation). When the strategist uses these to create an advantage, she has achieved the first level of competitive fit.

The firm must consider its own resources as well as its competitors' strengths, market conditions, and customers' desires as it chooses its weapons. Several points should be kept in mind. First, the strategist has to decide what the main weapon will be. If the strategist decides that product development is the main weapon, the firm should concentrate on strategies that use that weapon and downplay those that require strong price or service weapons. Research and development must be strong and product design effective for a product development strategy to work. Quality control becomes important to assure market acceptance.

In the last chapter I showed that the firm must satisfy at some minimum level all parts of the consumer bundle of desires. This principle also applies to competitive fit. Although the portfolio of competitive weapons must be focused, some minimum level of all weapons must be available. Even if the product is superb, a price set too high will draw the customer to an opponent.

Even in a single market, not all companies select the same weapons. The example from Chapter 3 of the two prefabricated housing firms comes to mind. Misawa succeeded with product differentiation, while Sekisui used service differentiation. This is the second point to keep in mind: there is no one best choice of weapons. The choice depends on the circumstances. The strategist must always keep in mind the company's individual competitive strengths.

No matter what the firm *intends* to accomplish, customers must *perceive* that the weapons actually create a competitive edge. A firm may try to compete with technical superiority, but if consumers do not see the firm as superior, the strategy is useless. Sony continued to use technology as its weapon to sell the Trinitron television even after other manufacturers had caught up with it. Sylvania's ads on U.S. television very effectively showed that consumers no longer saw Sony's picture as superior ("We beat Sony again," with sounds of excited Japanese offscreen).

Unless consumers perceive a clear difference, they will not be drawn to a firm's products. The consumer always makes the ultimate evaluation; the engineer's or salesperson's explanation is of minor importance. Consider the comments of Goro Noguchi, president of a fast-growing confectionary chain in Japan:

> The people who make and sell our company's candy believe it is better and more reasonably priced. But when you sell sweets, what you really want is for your customers to say that. Our salespeople might compare products and jump to the conclusion that our candy is of equal quality and a bit cheaper than that of our competitors, but it is not that simple. If we price our candy 10 percent cheaper, our customers will not get the impression that it is cheaper. We would have to price 20 or 30 percent cheaper before price becomes something the consumers cite as a major factor in purchase, at least in our business. (Industrial Bank of Japan, 1979)

The situation is similar in product function and supplementary services. Competitive edge has to be clearly recognized by customers. Too many firms try to create an edge without paying attention to the importance of consumer recognition.

THE CYCLE OF COMPETITIVE WEAPONS

In any one product or market segment, the appropriate weapons change over time. Usually product functions predominate at first, then supplementary services, and finally price. This cycle, shown in Figure 4–2, follows the life cycle of a product. During a product's early years, product differentiation is the driving force. As the period of fast market growth peaks, supplementary services become important. In the final stage of the cycle, prices can be lowered, and price becomes the main weapon.

When there is a choice, most managers agree that product function is the most desirable weapon, followed by supplementary services. In almost all industries, price competition is seen as the poorest alternative, since it lowers profitability. However, each of these types can be used successfully at different times. Price differentiation can open up new markets, as it did for Casio's digital watches; it can also be effective if it is based on considerably lower costs of production and operation. In general, however, it is a less effective weapon, because if a competitor is willing to accept losses, he can strike back immediately.

Fuji Photo's problems in entering the U.S. film market illustrate this problem. When the company cut the price of its paper to developers, Kodak followed suit and added an aggressive promotion campaign. When Fuji introduced high-resolution film in two speeds, Kodak did the same in four speeds. To make a dent in the market, Fuji took an area where Kodak could not respond easily, buying the rights to be the official sponsor for the 1984 Olympics. But Kodak bought a lot of TV commercial time to counter the threat (*Business Week,* Oct. 12, 1983).

It is harder for a competitor to counterattack when the weapon used is product function or supplementary services. A product that provides a new function is protected to some extent from counterattacks because of patent rights or accumulated invisible assets. With product differentiation such a desirable weapon, why do so many firms use the other alternatives? Why is price so frequently the competitive weapon when it is supposed to be the least effective? For several reasons firms cannot always choose the ideal weapon. First, its accumulated invisible and visible assets restrict the choice of weapons. Not all companies have strong distribution and service systems. And for some standard

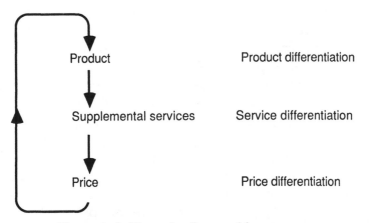

Figure 4–2. The cycle of competitive weapons

products, it is almost impossible to differentiate the product in a way consumers will recognize. It is hard to find a way to say that one company's sugar is different from any other company's sugar. Some types of differentiation are still possible; the company can differentiate with packaging design or size, or it can print the name of the supermarket on the bags as a service, for example.

More important, however, is that firms often overlook nonprice strategies. They get trapped into thinking that price is the only way to gain a competitive edge. Breweries that competed by lowering the price of a six-pack lost out to the companies that developed such new products as light beers and specialty beers and those that provided supplementary services such as packages that stay cold longer or mini-kegs that permit people to drink draft beer at home. Firms can usually find something other than price to use as a weapon, even in seemingly mature markets. At the very least, there should be some options for supplementary services.

Competitive pressures can sometimes affect the power of a weapon. If all the firms in an industry decide to use product differentiation to attract customers, each firm immediately tries to match the others. As soon as one manufacturer of videocassette recorders announced a new function, the other companies added a similar function. When this happens, firms switch to supplementary services, but that action is soon matched by opponents, and this advantage, too, is of short duration. At this point, price competition naturally becomes important, even though it produces few gains. If a strategist does some creative thinking, she can often find economical ways to develop effective nonprice differentiation.

That same kind of creative thinking is necessary to take advantage of the cycle of competitive weapons. A strategist will often find that a product has moved to a new stage in the cycle, requiring a change in weapons. A firm can either change weapons as the cycle progresses (preferably a bit before the change becomes clear to others) or keep its main competitive weapon (say, product function) and accept a weaker position when it becomes less effective in a given market. The firm can respond to market changes by skillfully combining particular products with the market segments in which this weapon can be used. For example, if product function has always been the firm's strength, it can react to the changed environment by sending a carefully planned mix of new products into a variety of new market segments. The ideal is to follow the first strategy of changing weapons, but there may not be enough resources to do that for all markets and all products simultaneously. If a firm's resources are spread too thin, its attempts are likely to fail.

Each strategy takes the cycle of competitive weapons into account to some extent. With the first approach, the firm changes its main weapon to respond to changes in the market. For a small firm with a narrow product line or only a few market segments, this may be the only possible response. That firm must prepare for changes before they occur. It must not only be first with the new product, but must also prepare to offer supplementary services as the cycle progresses. At a later stage, enduring a price-based competition requires streamlining operations. Of course, a new cycle may begin if the firm develops a new competitive product. Most companies that are successful initially with a single product and then expand operations must adjust their weapons to changes in the cycle.

A large company that operates in many markets may find it more difficult to change weapons. It is not easy to manage change when part of the organization is moving toward product differentiation while another part is abandoning it. Just as management costs set a limit on market segmentation, they also limit a firm's ability to change its competitive weapons in a wide variety of markets. If a strategist uses different strategies in various parts of the organization, her company's strength and corporate identity may be endangered.

Competitive conditions sometimes overwhelm these internal considerations. Yet, ironically, a large firm sometimes has to give internal factors top priority. For such a firm, responding with the strongest weapon at its disposal is the most appropriate strategy. It should deploy its strongest weapon in the market areas that are at the appropriate point in the cycle. The firm must identify the market segments for which its competitive weapons have the most power, then send products into each of these segments.

A good example is the Japanese consumer electronics industry. Each of the major firms has a primary weapon, but each still tries to selectively respond to the cycle. To oversimplify the situation, Sony emphasizes product differentiation; Matsushita, supplementary services; and Sanyo, price. If a new product like a VCR comes on the market, Sony is the first to market it, but as its product development weapon weakens over the cycle, the company must turn to new product areas. Matsushita's strong domestic sales network offers convenient purchase and service, as well as easily available financing. Matsushita's supplementary services become powerful at this stage of the cycle, and its VHS VCR system did not overtake Sony's Beta format until well into the cycle. Sanyo's weapon is price, based on its low-cost production system, so in the current maturing market, Sanyo will become increasingly competitive. Each firm uses all three competitive weapons, but each depends on a single strong element. Large organizations respond to the competitive cycle for individual products (strategy one), but they also move their resources between product and market segments to make the best use of a more stable, powerful primary competitive weapon (strategy two).

It sometimes pays to consider a strategy that does not follow the usual cycle of product first, services second, price third, especially when entering a new market. A firm may be able to create its own cycle. A new entrant, especially a previously unknown firm, may use the cycle of price, product, services. A low price strategy establishes the firm in the market. It then shifts to product differentiation, while gradually building a distribution system and a service network for the third stage.

Toyo Sash decided to use price for its initial entry into the aluminum window market. At the time it was a medium-sized company not known in the industry at all, but ten years later it was the top manufacturer in Japan. In the first years it acquired the nickname "discounter Toyo," as it pursued a price-based strategy. The company backed this strategy with aggressive plant and equipment purchases that lowered production costs. After establishing itself in the market, it came out with a series of new products that became hot sellers. The company is presently moving beyond product development to strengthen its distribution system. This has meant strengthening the sales force and moving toward direct sales for more of their product line. Their policies follow the above cycle almost exactly.

Japanese exports to the United States often show the same pattern, as can be seen in automobiles, copiers, televisions, and motorcycles. The firms choose a market segment that has the potential for high-volume sales, and attack it with a low price strategy. Once established, the firms begin to develop their distribution network (building invisible assets specific to the American market). They introduce a number of new products especially for those segments where they can expect to generate substantial profits. When their invisible assets have reached the appropriate level, they can offer supplementary services, thus attracting further customers. This sort of "newcomer cycle" is effective internationally as well.

These successful newcomers have two reasons for using this strategy: first, they are unknown when they enter the market, and, second, they do not have enough invisible assets to immediately develop new products that the market would accept. Consumers will not accept innovative new products from an unknown company; there is too much uncertainty about product quality.

There is no uncertainty about a low price; the customer does not have to use the product to see if the price is as advertised. Thus, price differentials can be a strong weapon for entering a new market where a firm and its products are not known. If some product differences go along with the low price, the strategy will be more effective; the key to success is still the strong price weapon. At a lower price, consumers will take a chance on the product. In doing so, they help build the invisible asset of brand recognition, which is necessary for product differentiation. It is probably not feasible to use product function as a weapon at this initial stage, when the firm does not have a wide range of invisible assets. If one thinks back to the poor image in American minds of Japanese products in the 1950s and the early 1960s, it is clear why the Japanese had to start with a low price strategy.

A firm that has already established its credibility and brand image in the market can take the more conventional approach, as can a firm that has an innovative product. Honda used its reputation as a supplier of small engines to establish itself in the lawnmower market with an innovative line that was both safe and easier to use.

Akai's new stereo receiver is another good example. That company had a good reputation as a manufacturer of tape decks, but it was not important in the stereo receiver market in the United States. Akai decided to introduce a new receiver model that incorporated microprocessor technology along with a display screen to show the functions controlled by the microchip. Without the company's previous reputation, such an unconventional approach would not have been accepted, yet the new model was hailed by a consumer magazine as the receiver of the future. Akai's invisible assets enabled it to deploy this product differentiation weapon. IBM's entry into personal computers followed the same pattern. When a firm can expect consumers to accept its product differentiation, the more conventional strategy and cycle is appropriate, even for a new entrant.

The most effective strategy for penetrating a new market is the one that is most likely to be accepted by consumers and that fits the cycle of competitive weapons. The success stories I have presented resulted from skillfully combining these two simple truths about competitive fit.

EFFICIENT PREPARATION OF COMPETITIVE WEAPONS

Markets and consumer desires determine what the best competitive weapon is. Every supplier in the market is considering these same problems, so the firm that creates the appropriate weapons earlier and more cheaply has a strong competitive edge. For example, a firm that foresees upcoming price competition and finds ways to lower its production costs will win that competition.

Lowering the cost of competitive weapons has to be a major corporate objective. This implies resource input. If a strategist wants to have supplementary services as the major weapon, the company must invest to strengthen the distribution channel, say. It must develop capable service and sales personnel as well as physical facilities. The return on the investment will come from the competitive edge created.

There are basically two ways to approach the decision on investing resources. A firm can use the resources it already has, but competitors lack, or it can allocate its resources differently. Even if a firm's resources are similar to those of other firms, it can concentrate those resources to create a key weapon. In either case, the competitive edge results from deploying resources differently from competitors. The process is illustrated in Figure 4–3.

The first approach uses such resources as brand name, an established distribution network, technology developed in other parts of the company, or even surplus physical resources (an idle factory). Conventional watchmakers lacked the computer chip technology that Casio used from its calculator division to enter the digital watch market. This approach is sometimes used successfully by small firms that must battle large competitors. A large firm may be unable to respond quickly to new market conditions because its decision-making processes are sluggish. It may be unable to keep up with the smaller firm that knows its market inside and out and has more up-to-date information. This is a major invisible asset for the smaller competitor. To efficiently create weapons the opponents lack, the strategist must carefully evaluate his assets and compare them with those of his competitors. Both visible and invisible assets are important.

The second method does not require a firm to have superior resources to its opponents. A different *concentration* of a relatively equal level of assets can still lead to successful creation of competitive weapons. If a firm and its opponents have the same financial resources, the firm can still create a pricing edge by applying most of its resources to plant and equipment purchases that reduce production costs, for example. The firm may have to sacrifice some product development or distribution efforts, but this is necessary to generate the competitive edge. Toyo Sash's investment in the early stages followed this pattern. It had no more resources than other firms and yet was able to create the necessary competitive edge and break out of the pack. Even in areas where a firm has chosen not to concentrate its resources, there may be some favorable spillover effects. Toyo Sash's chief executive officer, Kenjiroh Ushioda, had this comment: "Timing is important in investing in plant and equipment. We kept close tabs on housing start trends, and on the sales efforts of our company staff as we made those initial

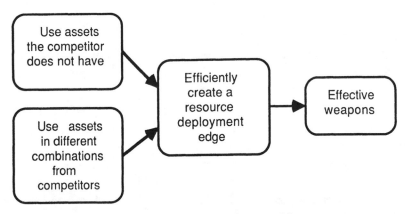

Figure 4–3. Efficient creation of competitive weapons

aggressive investments. Fortunately, our forecasts were right on the mark. We were able to operate at capacity, and costs came down. Lower costs led to increased sales, which kept our plants humming. We could confidently build our next plant under these conditions. It was a beneficial circle for us" (Tokunaga, 1979a).

A firm can create competitive weapons without having a superior level of resources to its competitors. It is extremely important for a firm to realize that as it looks for a favorable competitive position. It is easy to think of ways to be competitive when a firm has more resources than an opponent, but managers should remember that the second approach can be just as effective.

Protecting against Counterattack

Having achieved a strong competitive position, the strategist must consider how to protect that position from counterattack and avoid some of the fierce combat of the first level of competitive fit. Two approaches are available: reduce the incentives to counterattack and erect barriers making it hard to do so.

REDUCING INCENTIVES TO FIGHT BACK

A competitor's desire to counterattack is based on the expected benefits. If it feels that these benefits are small, the firm's position is secure.

One strategy for discouraging counterattacks can be called "self-inflicted wounds": the competitor finds that fighting back has damaging repercussions on his own strategy. Faced with such a situation, competitors lose their enthusiasm for battle. This frequently happens when a firm launches a substitute for a competitor's profitable main product. If the competitor responds with an additional product, he is further eroding the market for his current product; if he responds by cutting the price, it damages the profitability of his major product. When synthetic fabrics first hit the market, cotton textile manufacturers were slow to respond with improved cotton products or blends because they did not want to further disturb the market for their cotton textiles. A more current example is 8-millimeter home video. Producers of the larger VHS and Beta format VCRs are hesitant to get involved, since they are making good money in the home video market. New firms may thus be able to enter the 8-millimeter market without any immediate threat of counterattack.

Even if an established firm has for a period of time failed to make its position secure, it still can sometimes use its accumulated invisible assets, especially reputation, to effectively use the "self-inflicted wounds" strategy. It can use its accumulated resources to regain its position by initiating the counterattack rather than preventing it. A good case in point is Sony's recent move toward 8-millimeter video. Five years ago, Sony's commitment to the Beta format would have precluded an aggressive move into this new area. But as Matsushita's VHS system came to dominate the VCR market, Sony counterattacked by directly challenging the format through research and development in 8-millimeter technology. Since the company already has many of the resources necessary for developing and manufacturing these recorders, it has been able to proceed at a faster pace than an outsider that must first develop the resource base.

A regional air carrier can reduce its prices without necessarily calling forth a matching response from a national competitor. If the national firm matches the lower price, other parts of its route system may demand similar reductions. A national firm is thus being very rational when it fails to respond to regional price competition. It might try other strategies in the region, especially with supplementary services (such as a frequent flyer program), but it is not in a position to use the price weapon effectively in the regional market. Such cases are not uncommon. It pays to think about the potential benefits from markets that are relatively secure against counterattacks.

Another way to reduce incentives for competitors to fight back is to act first, anticipating their moves. The old Japanese saying, "Once a sake cup is full, you cannot get more in," expresses this strategy. If a company pours enough resources into the market, for example, through major investments in plant and equipment, there will be no room for competitors. If they try, they will just end up flooding the market with their resources. If a strategist expects very fast growth in market demand, it may pay to undertake a large-scale investment in plant and equipment before competitors can respond. For example, Sony, predicting a rosy future for its 3.5-inch floppy disk, announced a fivefold increase in production capacity at a time when IBM had not made clear its intentions for its next generation of personal computers (*Nihon Keizai Shimbun*, Aug. 13, 1984). That increase may have discouraged some firms from trying to erode Sony's dominant position in this market. Sony hoped that other firms would not match its investment, and its early decision made it harder for competitors to strike back.

If a company fails to make investments to meet potential future demand, it may face a strong challenge from new entrants. In postwar Japan the market shares in many industries changed drastically because the top firms did not have the capacity to meet surging demand. Those that invested were able to take the lion's share. In the worldwide competition between American and Japanese firms, American firms failed to protect their advantage by increasing production capacity to meet surging demand, leaving the door open for Japanese competitors. In the 1980 recession, when U.S. semiconductor manufacturers cut back on their investment in plant and equipment, the Japanese continued to invest aggressively, expecting strong future growth in demand. The demand for chips did bounce back, but because the American firms had not invested, they were not able to take full advantage of the increased demand, even as they remained profitable over the short term. The Japanese were able to establish a major market position. Having just completed their large-scale expansion, the Japanese firms were ready to step in and supply the market (Bylinsky, 1981).

American semiconductor firms have not repeated that error, but in many of the fast-growing markets in Japan a formerly dominant competitor has been overwhelmed when it permitted a smaller firm to penetrate the market. Nippon Electric in semiconductors, Bridgestone Tires, Toyo Sash, and Kirin Beer all took the competitive edge from larger firms in their respective industries by investing in anticipation of demand growth.

A firm may not have to actually invest substantial resources to prevent competitors from counterattacking. If competitors believe that the firm has a well-prepared plan to strike back and the commitment to carry out that plan, they may be dissuaded from even attempting an attack. This is the third approach to reducing incentives for counterattack. To drive that point home to competitors, a firm should be aggressive in carrying out its initial strategy, giving strong signals of its intentions by continually putting out new products or investing in plant and equipment.

A firm can publicize the policies it will take to defeat competitors, perhaps by concentrating salespeople in an area where it expects a counterattack. Or the firm can let it be known that it is preparing a product to compete with the mainstay product of a likely attacker. Of course, both firms realize that neither side would make a profit if the product were introduced into the market, but the signal performs a valuable function since only the competitor can stop this from happening.

These strategies may not dampen a competitor's enthusiasm for counterattacking. If the competitor decides to strike, both companies may be drawn into a no-win situation. In that sense, these strategies are a kind of bluff. A poker player who bluffs has to know that his opponent is likely to believe it; this is true in business as well. This requires knowing the opponent well. The corporate culture, the management's value system and attitudes, the firm's financial strength and invisible assets—all are important in judging whether the competitor is likely to counterattack.

BUILDING BARRIERS

The competing company may know how to counter a strategy, but if it cannot assemble the resources to carry out that counterattack, the firm is still secure. If the firm can control those resources, it will be more secure. The firm has to take some necessary resources out of the market before the opponent realizes their value.

An obvious example concerns the locations of key plants or stores. In many Japanese cities the number of potential locations for supermarkets is limited. Even in the United States, zoning often limits the number of locations. If a company wants to establish a national supermarket chain, it makes sense to acquire as many of these scarce land parcels as possible early on. Other firms will then find it hard to carry out a similar nationwide chain strategy because the land will simply not be available. Logging or mining rights and drilling permits all work the same way; early purchase forecloses competition. Similarly, if a firm vertically integrates the major suppliers of raw materials, a new entrant may have difficulty getting access to an assured supply. This increases the risk of the entrant's investment and is thus a barrier to counterattacks.

A firm considering entry into a field may find that a critical part is available only from a supplier closely tied or vertically integrated with another firm. The supplier might worry about losing his special relationship if he negotiates a supply contract with the new entrant, especially if the first firm has guaranteed to purchase a large portion of his output. One reason Boeing has signed subassembly contracts with firms in Japan and Italy is to stop or reduce the participation of these firms in the Airbus consortium, a major potential competitor for Boeing's dominant market position in commercial aircraft.

The opponent wants to use some of the first firm's assets, or other assets that will make an attack easier. If the firm can formally deny access to those assets, it has created another barrier against counterattack. Patents are the classic barrier of this type. Since the strategist does not know what direction the attack will come from, it is often wise to err on the side of too much patent protection. Long-term contracts with distributors or parts suppliers or capital investment in the distribution network can give the same protection. A new competitor cannot piggyback on a firm's distribution channel if the firm has this long-term commitment from the wholesale and retail outlets that handle its products. The new entrant will have to develop its own channels and pay the full cost of doing so.

Another technique for foiling counterattack is to keep competitors from getting access to needed resources. A firm can attempt to make success depend on access to resources it alone controls. If financing is a problem for most firms in an industry, and one firm has access to financing, it has an advantage over the others. If most of the firms in the industry are conservative and have a rather old-fashioned corporate culture, aggressive new product development may force them to counterattack with insufficient skills. In the United States, a good example of this strategy was the robotics firms' challenge to the small-scale craftsman-manned machine tool firms. Providing thorough, flexible service can also be an effective weapon against a traditional firm. Money in the first case and corporate culture in the second case are effective barriers because it is hard for a competitor to change the supply of these resources on a short-term basis.

Winning without Fighting

The third and most desirable level of competitive fit is keeping competitors from being opponents. The goal is to win without fighting by making potential competitors believe that the firm is not the enemy. The more competitors can be convinced of this, the fewer will enter the market in direct competition.

A good example is Seven Eleven Japan, a new entrant into the Japanese retail market in the early 1970s. It wanted to find good locations and expand quickly to take advantage of the new consumer taste for convenience foods. If Seven Eleven had tried to do this by having company-owned stores, which was the successful U.S. strategy, its entry would have been slowed substantially because the land was hard to acquire. Also, other retailers already owned the rights to sell liquor. Instead, it franchised the majority of its locations to corner grocery stores, rice shops, and liquor stores. These stores, hard-pressed at the time by the supermarket chains that were increasing their market share, were natural allies in Seven Eleven's penetration strategy.

The companies currently and potentially in a market need not be competitors if a firm successfully follows one of the following strategies: divide the market, prevent others from entering the market, or cooperate in the same markets. In the first strategy a firm decides not to compete and is content to operate in mutually exclusive segments or markets. This could include formal cartel agreements, which I do not treat here. Prohibiting entry is really an extreme case of dividing the market.

DIVIDING THE MARKET

One way to avoid competition is to choose segments that do not have strong competitors. This is a kind of differentiation strategy, keeping competitors at a distance. Smaller firms and specialty manufacturers often focus on market segments in which they have a strong advantage. Each firm finds a niche, and the market is divided among various manufacturers. This strategy works best if a segment with little competition also has some potential growth in demand. If the strategy succeeds, others will enter the market, but in the meantime, the pioneer can reap substantial profits. Even when competition intensifies, the first firm still has an advantage, and those assets—if maintained—may enable it to remain profitable.

Skylark, a Japanese family restaurant chain, took this approach. In 1970 the company decided to divest itself of its supermarkets and enter the restaurant business. *Hotel and Restaurant Weekly* (Dec. 2, 1977) gave the following account of the Skylark decision:

> In choosing the type of restaurant to open, President Chino had three criteria: potential for development of a large-scale chain; no

large firms or trading companies currently competing in that segment; a segment that, if successfully entered, would accumulate know-how that would make it hard for later entrants to compete successfully. President Chino, reflecting on that early period, commented, "Everyone I talked to urged me to go into the fast food business, but I thought we could not beat the general trading companies that were already competing in that segment."

It made sense for Skylark to avoid direct competition with fast-food joint venture of Kentucky Fried Chicken and Mitsubishi, the largest general trading company in Japan. President Chino's decision to open a chain of family restaurants put him in a segment that had hardly been explored in Japan and enabled him to build a competitive edge. The company opened two hundred outlets in nine years and almost doubled its sales each year for ten years.

The firm's strategy enabled it to accumulate invisible assets that were not currently available to many competitor firms. As soon as Skylark got into the market, it went right to work creating those invisible assets. The company created a thorough-going service system with extensive manuals to keep service levels high with a labor force of part-time workers. It created an extensive management control system for handling the increasing number of stores. A large central kitchen enabled operational efficiencies. With these and other efforts, they built up a fund of restaurant operating skills that was not easily matched by later entrants. Because of this solid foundation of invisible assets, Skylark did not encounter real competitive pressure until 1978, eight years after it began to develop this market.

A firm can get these benefits without opening an entirely new market. The strategist can choose a *segment* of an existing market that is not being well served by competitors, as the Japanese auto manufacturers did in the United States. The Japanese manufacturers concentrated on subcompact cars, an area of the market where the American big three manufacturers were not as strong.

Komatsu Forklift faced a similar situation in the Japanese market for these industrial vehicles. Although it was second only to Toyota, Komatsu's dealer network was inferior to that of the market leader. By concentrating on small, battery-operated lift trucks, Komatsu was able to maintain its market position and increase profits fourteen times in the five years from 1974 to 1979 (*Toyo Keizai,* Dec. 15, 1979). This kind of strategy does not fit the leading firm in an industry, but a second-rank or smaller firm can use it effectively, as can a medium-sized company in a market with larger firms.

Initially a strategist may select a small market segment; the firm can then avoid competition as it grows and develops invisible assets. The firm will eventually have to abandon this strategy, as will a firm that has developed a new market. The more successful the firm is, the more attractive entering that market becomes to others. Choosing to avoid competition initially does not guarantee lasting competitive success. Understanding this, the strategist will develop new strategies as the effectiveness of its market segmentation declines.

To successfully divide the market, the firm needs to answer three questions. What is the desirable segment? How can we get into that segment? How can we protect our competitive position if the strategy succeeds? The strategist should first identify the areas of the market where customer desires are not being met. A study of the strategies used by firms in entirely different industries domestically or in similar markets abroad may provide clues to potential markets, especially if the customers are similar to those in the markets being considered. Skylark studied the American chain restaurant business carefully.

The firm should find out why the segment has not been exploited. Although it may just have been overlooked, there are probably some specific reasons that other firms have not found it attractive. To develop that market segment, the firm must anticipate dealing with the problems that have discouraged other firms. Often an unconventional approach is the key. Skylark's success depended on its use of a central kitchen, its tight control of a part-time work force, and store leasing practices that were not common in the restaurant industry at that time. Skylark got these insights by carefully watching developments in other industries.

The third problem is to find ways to protect the market after its success becomes known. Skylark managed to extend the period of returns on the invisible assets it had developed. Keeping potential entrants out for a few more years will raise that return. It pays to find a market segment that is, as Skylark management put it, "hard to crack." Although such markets require more work to develop, success will yield higher returns. In a market that is easy to enter, a successful firm's position will be easy to counter as well. The best long-term plan—and the one that successful firms like Skylark have followed—is to accumulate invisible assets. The firm is then ready for the strong competition that will appear as its initial success becomes known.

PREVENTING ENTRY

The strategist must constantly work on ways to make entry into the firm's market segment difficult. Successfully keeping competitors from entering the market is a different way to win without fighting. Figure 4–4 illustrates the steps in creating barriers against competitors.

To shut out new entrants, a firm can either structure the market to lessen the benefits of entering it or erect barriers to entry. To lower the benefits of entering the market, firms can use limit pricing, develop excess capacity, or deny beachheads to new entrants. Limit pricing means setting a price lower than it would be if there were no potential competitors. That price is higher than the competitive price, the price with easy entry, but low enough that other firms cannot be profitable if they enter the market. Even though the market would bear a higher price, blocking potential competitors requires giving up some of that profit. The loss can be substantial. The lower the firm's costs relative to those of potential competitors, the less costly this strategy becomes.

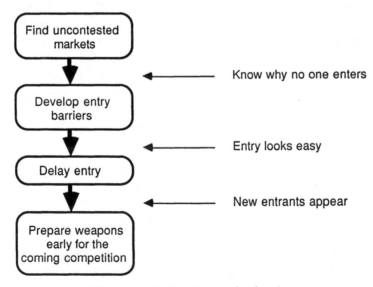

Figure 4–4. Erecting market barriers

If the entry threat becomes really strong, however, even firms with higher costs must consider this strategy, since a new competitor in the market will cause prices to drop even further.

Excess investment is essentially the same as the strategy for early investment discussed in the section on securing strategies against counterattack. If the firm has in place more than enough capacity to serve the market, a new competitor cannot expect to make much money there for quite a while. Denying a beachhead is an excellent strategy in this situation. A firm that establishes a beachhead in a market is ready to mount a challenge. Any attempted entry should be met with a strong response to drive the competitor out of the market. If the problem can be nipped in the bud, it will never grow large enough to threaten the firm. A strategist who knows how competitors may enter can prepare products to counter them. As soon as competitors announce their entry, the firm can reduce its prices. If they are using existing distribution channels, the firm can make attractive arrangements with wholesalers so that they have no time or space to handle the competitor's product. These are expensive strategies, but denying a beachhead may well be worth the cost.

The second way to win without fighting is to erect entry barriers. Entry barriers are similar analytically to counterattack barriers, but there is an important distinction. Entry barriers are of two types: those derived from differences in the level of invisible assets (technology, brand image, raw material sources) of the current participant and potential entrants, and administrative barriers (patents, currency controls, government regulations favoring existing participants). Most administrative barriers support the established firm.

Different techniques are used to erect these two types of barriers. Creating administrative barriers, such as Japan's effective shutting out of foreign investment until 1970, requires political action. Existing barriers (such as research and development to get patent protection, or "Buy American" contracts that foreign steel manufacturers are not permitted to bid on) can be used effectively.

On the other hand, a firm can build effective barriers through the accumulation and application of invisible assets. The firm must try to make sure that its internal resources are accessible and that they do not become available to competitors. It must also try to influence overall market supply conditions so that potential competitors are denied access to essential resources.

The strategist trying to erect these barriers must keep in mind two points: the *unpredictability* and the *inevitability* of competitors entering the market. The fast pace of technological change makes it extremely difficult to forecast where the next opponent will come from, which makes it hard to know how long the existing barriers will be effective. Competitors enter the market from unexpected directions.

A firm must always assume that competitors *will* enter the market, even as it tries to erect effective barriers. Entry barriers will *delay* entry, but they are unlikely to wipe out all potential entrants. A firm that thinks it has permanently blocked all competitors will pay a high price later when a competitor comes up with a new competitive weapon.

COOPERATING

A third way to avoid having competitors be opponents is through co-operation. Firms can find many ways to cooperate within the antitrust laws. For instance, all participants can join an association that represents the interests of that industry. In Japan such associations provide a forum for discussion of common problems. Firms decide to cooperate because it is in their individual interests to do so. Cooperation may increase the demand for a product, as was true with the advertising of Florida orange juice, and it may lower the level of uncertainty through discussion and exchange of information.

Positive results are most likely when firms cooperate on technology and on product standards. The half-inch videotape recorder case is a good example. The various companies in the industry did *not* choose to cooperate on a single standard, and the public was faced with two competing systems, Matsushita's VHS and Sony's Beta. As a result, consumers were confused. If the two companies had cooperated to reduce this confusion, they could have concentrated on expanding demand for their products. The VCR industry has seemingly learned its lesson; more than a hundred manufacturers around the world have agreed to a single standard for 8-millimeter video, the next stage in this market.

The decision to license a firm's technology or other invisible asset is in effect a decision to cooperate with competitors on technology. Oftentimes it is the best strategy. Japan Victor and Matsushita, two electronics firms, have for a long time worked together to build a set of firms that use its VHS system for VCRs. That cooperation, based on a license to use the VHS system, included technology sharing.

Their VHS system has sold considerably better than Sony's rival Beta system, which Sony has tried to develop and sell almost entirely on its own.

Technology sharing by cooperating firms can generate several benefits. The products can be advertised together to help reduce consumer uncertainty. Standardization is welcomed by consumers and spurs demand, especially at the early stage of product development. Consumers tend to postpone purchasing if they see a number of similar but incompatible products in the market.

Sometimes technology sharing can give a firm access to a large group of customers it would otherwise not have. Many users who get acquainted with the firm through a particular product will remain customers for other products later on. Technology sharing expands the customer base. The decision to cooperate is a decision between having a large market share in a limited market and having a smaller share in a substantially expanded market. Usually the larger market is worth the reduced share.

The third benefit of technology sharing is that improvements flow back to the firm. Each firm sees different uses for the same technology, or different possible extensions of it. Each company, with its unique strengths, can correct some of the weak points; as a result, all firms gain. Cooperation can also be beneficial in other areas besides technology.

As with most classification schemes, it would be unusual for a firm to choose a strategy that is one of the pure types mentioned above. A pair of firms may divide one market between them, compete in another, and cooperate in yet a third. The Japanese aerospace industry provides a good example. Each of the major firms is a prime contractor for one type of military aircraft, but they compete in helicopters and engines and cooperate on supply contracts with Boeing for the 767.

It may seem paradoxical that a chapter titled "Competitive Fit" ends with a recommendation for cooperation. There is a very significant lesson here: competitive fit should not be considered as just battling with competitors. Winning without fighting and cooperation with competitors are just as important as the more conventional elements of competitive fit.

Although firms may decide to cooperate with competitors in many

areas, in the last analysis they are still competitors. Cooperative arrangements do not last indefinitely, as may be appropriate for today's
rapidly changing business environment. Technological innovations appear constantly, and business activities have become increasingly international. World political conditions continue to change the shape of
the business environment. Cooperating firms can use the spillover effects from cooperation internally, knowing that in tomorrow's environment each firm will have to find new partners to continue the dynamic effects of this type of arrangement.

Technological Fit

Chapter 5

Technological fit involves a struggle with nature rather than people. The firm achieves technological fit as it discovers the potential of nature's untapped resources, turns them into technology, and then applies that technology through new products or new manufacturing processes. Unearthing the potential hidden in nature is the first stage, *technological discovery*. Even more than competitors or customers, nature can affect the environment in which the company operates, and that effect is surrounded by uncertainty. Through technological discovery, a firm must come to terms with nature if it is to achieve environmental fit.

The second stage, in which new technology is incorporated into new products and marketed, is *commercialization*. Without the commercialization stage, discovery gains the firm, and society, little. The technology must fit within the firm's societal framework; otherwise it has no economic effect. A new-born technology cannot survive without a social foundation and the potential for consumer demand. Social conditions are a deciding factor in whether a new technology will be profitably incorporated into a firm's activities. A strategy has to guide the organization's various efforts toward both technological discovery and commercialization. When it succeeds, and the firm's direction matches the technological trends of the firm's environment, we say the strategy has achieved technological fit.

The paradox of technology is that it is both uncertain and logical. Future technology is always uncertain, and yet after it is brought to light its logic is clear. To put it differently, technology development is a mixture of chance and inevitability.

Technology is always uncertain before development succeeds. No one set out to invent the transistor. Bell Labs researchers William

Shockley and Walter Brattain came upon its basic principle during their studies in solid state physics. Conversely, many research and development projects fail even though they are well endowed with both financial and human resources. An American company, Trilogy, well funded by venture capital and headed by George Amdahl, a proven veteran of the competitive computer industry, had to give up its attempt to make a computer chip one hundred times the size of the current integrated circuit (Hayes, 1984). The creation of new technology is uncertain and serendipitous; it is impossible to precisely predict its timing or nature.

Once discovered, technology has a logic; that is, we can explain precisely why the technology accomplishes what it does, and in clear, analytical terms. After the serendipitous discovery of the transistor, the new logic of the semiconductor was unraveled and was clear to everyone who understood this field. That logic then formed the basis for the series of new technologies used in the integrated circuit industry. A useful technology is always a *ring* of logic. Each bit of knowledge must be in place to create the ring and render the technology functional. At various points in the development of semiconductor technology, finding out how to draw ever denser lines on the chip held up development, even though other elements necessary for the next jump were in place. In this sense technology is strictly logical. If one piece is missing the system will not have the ring of logic necessary for it to function.

The people who search out these technologies cannot know what they will find until they are finished; they must live with uncertainty *during* the process and assume the risk involved. Looking back later, they may admire the elegantly simple logic of the new technology and wonder why it took them so long to see it. Yet without each piece in place, that elegant simplicity cannot be seen. These two apparently contradictory characteristics of technology are thus in reality consistent. Uncertainty before the project succeeds is replaced by logic after the technology has been brought to light.

Technological fit is often defined too narrowly as finding ways to develop products that fit with *existing* technology. But that does not enable the firm to come to grips with both the uncertainty and the hidden logic in nature. In dealing with the uncertain nature of technology, a firm can choose a passive response, perhaps undertaking a series of parallel projects in developing new technology to spread the risk. Or it can choose a strategy that actively tries to reduce uncertainty. Or it can seize the opportunity to identify the logic of technologies hidden in nature. Because technology is uncertain, the strategy may have to serve as a lever of certainty to guide people. I will also discuss various aspects of fit (passive, active, leveraged) in this chapter.

Technological Uncertainty

Until technology has been put to use, three types of uncertainty are important to the strategist: discovery does not always result from technology development efforts; markets do not always accept products from new technology; and newly developed technology can become obsolete. Uncertainty is present in any effort to discover the secrets of nature. The results can never be forecast; the process is inherently risky and requires continuous struggle. From the various possible sets of logic, a firm must choose the one that meets its technological development goals. At first, many good logic systems may seem appropriate. How much time it will take and what invisible assets will be required are never clear beforehand. In fact, there is no assurance of success. It is like sailing a ship into uncharted waters. It is impossible to know whether treasure abounds or disaster lurks. By the time the firm goes through the learning process and finds which elements are necessary to complete the ring of logic, it may be too late to make the resulting product a commercial success; at the least, delays will be encountered.

Even after the uncertainty of technology development has ended, market acceptance uncertainty remains. The new technology must still meet a market demand, which can change quickly. Four-channel stereo and video disks are recent examples of excellent technologies that were not well received by consumers. When RCA decided to withdraw from the video disk player market, it cited unexpected consumer preference for recording as well as playback. The technology to create the personal computer was available for years before Apple and other pioneering firms defined the particular features and price structure that would lead to consumer acceptance.

Uncertainty also exists about the lifespan of any technology. Competitors are also challenging nature to develop new technology; they may find some new logic that will erode the technological asset base a firm has carefully built up. As Chiyoji Misawa, president of Misawa Homes, said, "There is always a danger that a new technology pops up without warning and changes your industry completely. It often comes from companies you never expect" (Misawa, 1984).

Companies must learn to deal with these three types of uncertainty. The following strategies are useful: maintaining a deep pool of core technological assets, combining the different types of technology risk, conducting more and earlier experimentation in the field, and keeping up with technology trends.

CREATING A CORE TECHNOLOGY

No strategist can expect to cover all the technological possibilities; there must be a focus, a core technology. With an established core, the firm has an anchor against the uncertainties of technological discovery and commercialization. Without that focus, a firm may spread its resources too thin. People will become indecisive under the cover of avoiding excessive change. A core technology also reduces the risk of obsolescence by making the portfolio of technologies more flexible.

The selection of a core technology can be a crucial strategic decision. Nippon Electric chose microelectronics and optical electronics as its core technologies. As Michiyuki Uenohara, head of research and development at Nippon Electric, warned, "If you focus only on individual product technologies, that will often lead to major strategic errors." He said that a strategist may be tempted to develop all the new products that show a potential for success. But to do so, a firm would have to slash efforts on technologies that could be important later or skimp on the accumulation of invisible assets. Uenohara continued:

When you draw up a matrix of the individual technology requirements necessary to develop a series of new products or to meet new market demands, you will often find that these products or demands share a set of basic technology requirements . . . Once you successfully assemble this set of technology elements that can work together in each of the several specific product areas, you can assign research groups to do long-term research and development on this set of basic technologies, . . . [which] are then grouped to form a core technology for the firm. Basic technology will change with the pattern of consumer desires and with advances in technology, but the core technology will not change in ten to twenty years. (Imai et al., 1983)

Ajinomoto, a diversified chemical and condiments firm, chose amino acid technology as its core technology, which enabled it to diversify its product lines. The basic technology for producing amino acids, originally developed for its condiments business, changed over time from extraction from plants to chemical synthesis and finally to fermentation. Each of these new procedures in amino acid technology gave the company new opportunities for diversification. Each technological breakthrough seemed to create new opportunities for further growth. Artificial sweeteners, soft drink products, and pharmaceuticals were some of the products that resulted from Ajinomoto's deep accumulation of its core technology.

A firm may choose its technological core not only along product lines but also along the lines of its operations mission, focusing on technology for product development, or on production, or on distribution. The appropriate core need not be fancy; mundane production technology makes money for Sanyo even as Sony steals the product development headlines. A firm can focus on mass production or on production of a wide variety of products, but a clear core technology is always necessary.

Conditions in the market often dictate the appropriate focus. If the company decides to use product features as a competitive weapon, product development technology has to become the core. In consumer electronics Sony has followed this strategy successfully, introducing innovative products from the portable tape recorder in the 1950s to the Walkman and audio disk in the 1980s. Other firms, content to let these pioneers develop the product, enter the market later, when the product has been standardized and they can use price as a competitive weapon. For these companies, production technology is the core.

Focusing on a core technology does not mean that the company can afford to ignore other areas; all the elements must mesh. An acceptable level of technology in product development, production, and distribution must be maintained no matter which area the company focuses on.

What makes a firm willing to accept the risks to develop technology?

Many excellent, well-intentioned efforts fail, and those that do succeed still take a long time. Potential future profits are an obvious incentive. A charismatic leader can carry others along by the strength of his personality and beliefs, registering strong support for a project. The romance of technology can exert a similar pull on the people in the organization. The strategist should keep this romantic element in mind as he plans a core technology.

A proposed technology must give those who work on it a dream, something to aim at. This might be the impact the new technology will have on society or the challenge of working at the frontiers of technology. The target should be hard to reach but one that can be visualized; then the dream will help drive the development effort.

Leaders of advanced technology projects often talk in such terms. In 1953 Masaru Ibuka of Sony was driven by the romance of the then-new transistor technology to try to improve the high-frequency response in radios. Honda's motorcycle success was based on the romance of winning what was then the most prestigious motorcycle race in the world, the Mann's Island race. Within five years of announcing, in 1954, that it would participate, Honda had improved their technology enough to enter the race and win a prize. Two years later they won the championship. Soichiro Honda's dream of world-class motorcycle technology had been realized.

Such a dream can drive employees to accept the risks that go with technology development. When the technical experts are still in the dark about the results of their efforts, the dream is like the beacon of a lighthouse, indicating that successful passage is possible. This gives them the strength to endure the adversities of the voyage. If people were like machines, spitting out technological results like so many assembly-line products, romance would have no worth. Because they are not, romance can be part of strategy. The romantic element can serve as a springboard to launch a new technology. Toshio Ikeda, known as the computer genius who made Fujitsu a strong computer company, put the issue to his colleagues this way: "I want you to become people who are highly energized, people who can feel deep emotion. Once you have this, you have the strength to create anything you want. It does not matter if you are talking about music or computers. Nothing starts unless you have been deeply moved. Once you have been deeply moved, there is something dynamic already stirring within you" (*Nikkei Business,* Mar. 22, 1982).

COMBINING TECHNOLOGICAL RISKS

Combining several paths of technological development can often reduce the overall risk, just as a product/market portfolio reduces the risk in customer fit. A number of parallel development methods can be used to achieve a single research objective. Since the strategist cannot know in advance which method will succeed, he will try several at once to reach the desired goal.

Combination strategies work best with development risk and market risk. One strategy that can deal with these risks as well as with obsolescence risk is a combination of supporting and destructive technologies. By *supporting* I mean technologies that extend the life of the firm's current products and existing technology. In contrast, *destructive* technology reduces—often to zero—the value of existing products and technologies. Masaru Masujima, head of research and development at TDK, the leading manufacturer of magnetic tape, coined the expressions. In his words, "For TDK, we can do things to further improve the quality of our tape (metal vacuum deposition tape technology). This is a supporting technology. If we develop optical recording technology, that is destructive technology. By developing such a destructive technology in our laboratories, however, we can be prepared if our existing tape technology becomes obsolete" (*Nikkei Business,* Mar. 22, 1982).

This combination does more than diversify risk; it gives the strategist a lever for making technology development more effective.

When both supporting and destructive technologies are developed simultaneously, competition is created between the two. This works to both speed up the pace of improvements to existing technology and increase the pace of development of new destructive technology. As existing technology is improved, it provides a moving target for the new, destructive technology. This then stimulates the development of new technology. Figure 5–1 shows the relationships among the types of technologies.

The stimulus from new technology in improving existing technology is much more important than might be thought. Improvements in existing products are more likely to succeed than completely new products, and the economic gains are far greater than commonly believed. Improvements resulting from pressure on existing technology may be an unexpected by-product of destructive technology development. The firm may consciously exploit this driving mechanism to get better supporting technology at the same time that it challenges the system with destructive technology.

Lowell Steele (1983), long-time manager of research and development at General Electric, had this to say about these benefits: "New technology constantly chases the moving target of conventional technology, which is itself goaded to accelerated improvement by the threat. The new technology rarely catches up. In fact, one of the most important economic benefits of innovative activity is the stimulus it gives to conventional technology."

To create this dynamic interaction between supporting and destruc-

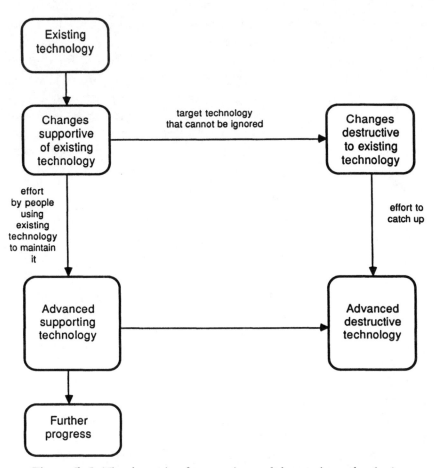

Figure 5–1. The dynamic of supporting and destructive technologies

tive technologies is no easy task. It is hard to get an organization to accept efforts to create destructive technologies because they seem to deny the value of the company's current technology. People instinctively reject technologies that might destroy the firm's current environment. This may be one reason American vacuum tube manufacturers were not able to ride the wave of new semiconductor technology when it engulfed their existing technology in the 1950s.

EXPERIMENTING IN THE FIELD

In dealing with technological uncertainty, the firm has to go through a process of experimentation or learning. One technique the strategist can use to reduce uncertainty is "premature" or "excessive" experimentation in production for actual sale. Experimentation and learning do not take place only in the lab. Production people have to start making a product to get the technology ready for the shop, and marketing people have to actually sell the product to get feedback from the market's response. Often, test production and extensive market surveys are no substitute for early and extensive market participation.

Experimental commercialization accelerates improvements in technology. Market experimentation means getting a product that is being developed out of the sterile lab and into the market. It means selecting a target market and testing for product acceptance. Doing this early and often makes clear to everyone in the firm the final goal of their effort—market acceptance. It also provides invaluable feedback at a stage when adjustments can still be made.

Sanyo is a world leader in solar cell technology. That company's development of amorphous solar cells is a good example of the potential of early commercialization. Competitive edge in this market comes from the heat exchange efficiency of the cells. Sanyo chose to commercialize its design even before it had reached a high level of efficiency, using the cells first in watches and calculators. The head of research and development at Sanyo, Hiroshi Yamano, gave the following rationale for the decision:

Commercialization is one key way to promote improvements in technology. You have to clarify your target market and the path you will use to commercialize the technology. This forces people to increase the pace of development. This is why we are commercializing solar cells with only 3 percent efficiency. We picked products—watches and calculators—that can run even with these low-efficiency cells. Had we been more conservative and waited until efficiency had reached 5 percent, the development pace would have been much slower. (Uchihashi, 1980a)

The information the engineers obtained both from the production crew and from the market as Sanyo put these solar cells into their products was much richer than lab information alone could have been.

Some have labeled the experimentation stage the troubleshooter stage. Time after time, the lab may turn out technology that is supposed to work, but only when production is actually begun is it known if there are problems. It is often a big leap from the logic in the lab to a workable technology. At each step, problems have to be analyzed and remedies prescribed. Only through this laborious process can commercially meaningful technology be born.

Troubleshooting is the key to success in the current high technology environment. Getting employees to deal with problems early and in a variety of contexts gives the firm a head start. A firm that experiences a lot of problems is ironically in the best position to finish the technology race in front. Early commercialization can often help achieve this goal.

It is important to find opportunities to learn from experience. The volume production stage may provide such opportunities. Technical problems always occur at the start of volume production. Areas in the production process itself may cause trouble. As these problems are solved, the technology becomes more hardened. The experience effects of troubleshooting are well illustrated in the semiconductor industry, where production innovations have continually reduced costs. To get the benefits of cumulative production, early commercialization is necessary.

RUNNING WITH THE TRENDS

Even with the high levels of uncertainty in technology, a strategist should be able to read the general trends. Even in such an uncertain technology as semiconductors, trends can be seen. Every two years the density of the chips has increased by a factor of four. New types of chips, labeled CMOS, which use less energy and generate less heat, are becoming more important each year. It is hard to know in advance *how* the industry will achieve the next level of chip density. The required technologies are not clear, nor are the means by which firms will eventually hurdle that density barrier. But the trend is there, and the pattern is likely to be repeated.

Some longer-term trends can also be discerned. Most specialists see optical electronics as the next major area of useful technology. Further down the road, a mixture of biotechnology and electronics seems promising. Actual technology does not follow a trend exactly; the trial and error process of technological development follows a zigzag pattern along the general direction of the trend of technological change, as shown in Figure 5–2.

A strategist, of course, has to read current trends correctly and act quickly on that information. Not all trends will be obvious to everyone who looks at the market. Of a series of tendencies that appears, only one may turn out to be the actual trend. If the strategist does not read that trend correctly, the firm's competitive position can be seriously weakened.

It is generally agreed that the Swiss watch industry ignored this rule

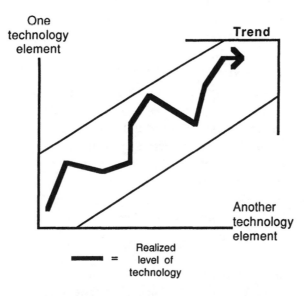

Figure 5–2. Zigzag pattern of technology trend development

in responding to the integrated circuit technology. Because they did not take advantage of new technological opportunities, the Swiss fell from a 90 percent global market share to less than 20 percent in less than three decades. With no significant electronics industry, Swiss watchmakers found it difficult to gather information on the trends that were to buffet the industry and failed to read the signs of change implicit in integrated circuit technology.

Technology may follow a natural path. As the flow of technology continues, however, it will sometimes encounter natural barriers. These may loom so large that they obscure the overall trend. The technology of automobile engines has been characterized by increases in combustion efficiency. Automobile manufacturers are always trying to increase that efficiency, but for many years the engines have remained about the same; development has hit a barrier. To surmount that barrier, firms are trying to develop ceramic engines, which, if successful, will increase engine efficiency dramatically. Problems remain in both the development and the production of a high-quality, mass-produced ceramic engine. If these problems can be overcome, however, the technology will continue the trend toward more efficient combustion engines.

The second point is that it is essential to constantly ride with the trend. If a firm decides to stop for a while or hesitates to go with the trend, it may be hard to catch up.

Trends emerge because the development efforts of many people occur within the same logical framework. Providing a single logic within which everyone must work helps create interaction and deep probing. The semiconductor logic is a clear example; the efforts of many researchers gradually reduced the uncertainty within the overall framework. Most people are working from the same assumptions and share a common core of knowledge. A discovery by one person may give others a hint that enables them to hit on a new idea as well. Knowing about other people's progress stimulates each researcher to make new discoveries. Each bit of technology makes the next bit easier to accumulate. A firm that keeps up with the trend can capitalize on this dynamism.

If a firm stops adapting to the dynamic nature of the technology trend, it may be left behind permanently, for it is not easy to rebuild the earlier momentum. To stay with the trend, a strategist should commit the firm's resources to research and development, to investments in facilities, and to enlargement of operations.

Nippon Electric, the world's largest producer of integrated circuits, has constantly met these challenges, staying right with the trends in semiconductor technology. Until the early 1970s, it was behind Hitachi and ran neck and neck with Toshiba within Japan, but it had a reputation for keeping up with the trends. The head of the semiconductor division, Atsuyoshi Ouchi, described the competitive changes after the 1973 oil shock this way: "We seem to come out of each recession with a larger market share. We never cut back on research and development expenditures or on facilities investment just because we were currently in a recession. We still pour money into the facilities and people, continuing to hire technical people even in those tough times. The results from these carefully thought-out efforts gave us the power to overtake Hitachi and become the largest integrated circuit producer in Japan" (Nakagawa, 1983).

Technological Interdependence

The second essential characteristic of technology is its internal interdependence. Each element in technology can function only if it is tied to the surrounding elements by a particular logic. The firm must learn to use this logic of interdependence in developing its strategy.

Every technology contains related elements and is surrounded by additional related elements. These relationships are of three types: between technology components, between individuals who deal with the technology, and between the technology and society. The essential components of a company's technology portfolio, for example, engine technology and suspension technology in automobiles, are obviously related. The relationships can be classified in a number of ways, such as materials technology, electronics technology, and mechanical technology. No matter what the classification, the technological components must be interdependent in order to achieve technological fit. Of course, the definition of a single technology can be as fine as one wants to make it.

The second group of relationships is among those who work with the technology, including engineers, the company's work force, suppliers, and distributors. If these diverse groups, each with its own characteristics and type of technical knowledge, cannot work together at some level, contradictions will develop within the organization and the technology will not function.

The third set of relationships involves society. The technology and those who work with it exist within wider social contexts, some of which may be far removed from technology. Technology has no value until society accepts it. For example, it took a substantial period of time for consumers to understand the value of auto emission devices, even though the technology was available. Consumers still have not accepted the safety and effectiveness of airbag restraints, though again the technology has been available for quite a while. Social and market factors have to be included in the interdependence logic.

TECHNOLOGY LEVELING

Strategy must establish mutual interdependence among the technology components as well as between the people and the technologies. The strategy must integrate the weak as well as the strong elements of the technology. The weakest links dictate the pace at which technology can proceed, since all are interdependent. As with a mountain climbing party, the speed of the slowest member dictates the pace. The strategy must enable the weak elements to progress at adequate speed, rather than simply accelerating the strong elements. This is called technology leveling.

A technology team may develop a good product, but unless the people who commercialize and market it understand its technology, they will not be able to market it effectively. Only after the firm has a grasp of all the essential elements can it bring the product to commercial life. For example, a Japanese sewing machine manufacturer tried to diversify into consumer electronics products, such as microwave ovens, but its sales force did not have the technical skills to service the new product, and the effort failed. Xerox and Exxon both introduced sophisticated office automation products but were not successful; they were not able to tie the sales of those products into their wider corporate strategy.

In contrast, Toray, a large Japanese textile firm, successfully applied technology leveling. Before World War II the company had begun research on nylon, using a process different from Dupont's. When Dupont's nylon technology became available, Toray made a tremendous financial commitment to license it, knowing that it had the necessary resources to take advantage of this epoch-making change in textile technology. If it was developing its own nylon process, why license? The response illustrates Toray's approach to technology:

> With the license, we could get related technologies in filament processing, weaving, and dying. We needed Dupont's permission to import much of the related machinery. Some countries base their patent laws on chemical compounds rather than on process. Without the license, we would have been limited in export potential. The contract stipulated that we had the right to produce nylon using their process. We did not get detailed nylon process know-how from Dupont. We did, however, obtain detailed process know-how in other areas (spinning, processing, dying, finishing). This of course helped to expedite the commercialization process. (Moriya, 1978)

A firm can function only if the technologies of product development, production, and distribution are on the same level. If workers' skills do not match the level of technology, the interdependence logic does not work. If a firm is developing a production system based on using unskilled workers, it makes no sense to require those workers to carry out operations that demand a high degree of precision. Selecting a product line without considering the abilities of the workers and the production system will result in a high defect rate that will doom the product in the market. As I described earlier, Matsushita's use of dry cell batteries as an initial product for overseas production is consistent with technology leveling. Matsushita started with a particular product line (batteries) and a given resource level (unskilled labor), but it planned for changes in the scope of its operations over time. Eventually the overseas plants trained and used skilled labor and developed a more diverse product line.

Unless a firm plans to make all parts in-house, outside parts manufacturers and other subcontractors are also an important element in the overall logic of technology. A company needs to cooperate with suppliers and work aggressively to upgrade their technology. Japanese automobile assemblers are well known for providing technological assistance to their major suppliers, but any firm that subcontracts a large portion of work while striving for a high level of technology must do the same. When Boeing chose Fuji Heavy Industries to produce light composite structures for its 767 plane, it made sure that the Japanese firm understood the necessary technology to reliably build these parts.

Japanese firms have used this leveling principle effectively, which is one reason they have been so successful in world markets. When a Japanese firm moves toward commercialization, it does not just start on research and development. It simultaneously develops the production technology and worker skills necessary for the product to succeed; it makes sure all the elements of technology are at the appropriate level.

Another element in the success of Japanese firms has been the upgrading of suppliers' technology, bringing it to a level necessary for success in world markets and giving the supplier firms the skills to develop their own invisible assets in technology. From the Korean War to the mid-1960s, smaller firms received substantial technology assistance from larger firms and developed their own technologies as well, especially in parts production and services. Long-term arrangements enabled the large firms to pressure the smaller ones to meet high standards. The larger firms saw the smaller suppliers as closely related to them rather than as independent adversaries. By 1970 these smaller firms could develop their own technologies, enabling the large firms to engage in aggressive overseas expansion.

My earlier emphasis on a core technology may sound inconsistent with technology leveling, but there is a logic connecting the two. Technology leveling dictates the pace, but the core technology is what holds the system together. A mountain-climbing party climbs at the pace of its slowest members, but the leader sets the direction, just as the core technology focuses the overall effort.

Figure 5–3 illustrates the point that a firm's technology should be T-shaped. The technological core gives a solid foundation for a wide set of well-balanced, related technologies. Each firm has a different arrangement of the elements within the T. For Sony the core is product development; for Sanyo, production technology. Each firm has a series of related technologies that complete the T; Sony has production technology to exploit its new product ideas, and Sanyo engages in product development to make its core production technology effective.

THE BILLIARD EFFECT

When one part of technology changes, no other part will remain stationary; this is the billiard, or chain reaction, effect, another kind of interdependence. The strategist must understand that changes in one element affect the relationships among all the technology elements. Especially when her firm initiates the changes, the strategist has to plan carefully to make sure the billiard effect takes place; otherwise the full effect of technological innovation is never realized.

No matter where a technological innovation starts—from a firm's own efforts or from another firm—the billiard effect works its way through the system. It may have totally unexpected repercussions. The strategist must be on the alert for technological advances over a wide and ever-changing set of areas. Developments in liquid crystal displays and semiconductors changed watchmaking. Advances in synthetic fibers transformed the textile industry into one based on chemical technology. Future advances in storage battery technology could cause the automobile industry to look more like the electrical equipment industry. A strategist never knows where or how the wave of new technology will change the industry.

Up to this point, the examples have been of changes in one technology influencing another technology. These are the easiest billiard effects to observe, but other, more subtle effects can be just as significant. The office automation revolution and the widespread use of word processors equipped with communication facilities have greatly reduced the demand for printing services, for instance.

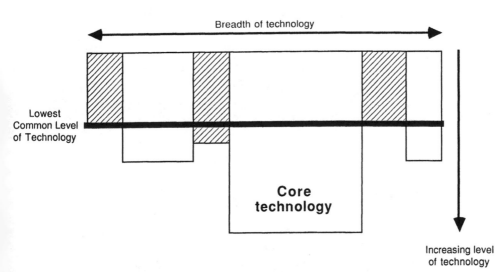

Figure 5–3. The T-form for technology

The financial services industry has been revolutionized by changes in an unexpected source, computer-based communication. Financial intermediaries match lenders with borrowers. With computers reducing the cost of information exchange, financial services cannot help but be affected. Nomura Securities has been in the forefront of these changes. Setsuya Tabuchi, president of that firm, put it this way: "Everyone wants in on the new order in financial markets. The basic reason for the revolution is the computer. That gives them the initial impetus. If you want to settle accounts, you no longer have to use a regulated banking system. With computers, security firms can easily do this business that was formerly reserved for banks" (Tabuchi, 1984). Technological innovation in seemingly unrelated areas can influence the *operations* of markets and the *functions* of particular markets.

The billiard effect can reach the firm through yet another route. Technology that affects people's lives outside the company can force changes in strategy. With improved transportation and communication links to smaller cities, people in Japan have moved away from metropolitan areas. In the United States, some software developers live deep in the Cascade Mountains and send their results to Silicon Valley firms electronically. Such changes in living patterns will change patterns of demand for products and will influence the composition of the labor force in each area.

If a technological change hits a barrier, however, no further billiard effects are generated. When a firm expects to take advantage of repercussions from new technology, it must make sure that no barriers are in the way. Those barriers can be in the technology elements, in the market, or in society. To make American computer software acceptable to East Asian markets, firms had to find ways to make the programs run with Chinese characters. As integrated circuits became more dense, this barrier was lowered, and sales of software by both Japanese and U.S. suppliers took off.

In the video disk player market, the barrier was the small number of movies and other disks available. Pioneer, the first manufacturer of laser players, put a lot of effort into increasing the number of disks. Robotics provides an example of a societal barrier. In the United States the introduction of robots has met resistance from labor unions, whose members fear loss of jobs. In Japan, on the other hand, the robots were first used for welding jobs in smaller firms. Welding was not an attractive job, and long-term employment was never important in this nonunionized portion of the Japanese economy.

When such impediments are removed, the repercussions continue, and the technological changes acquire a life of their own. The strategist must decide where the barriers are, which barriers might be easiest to surmount, and which barriers are crucial to allowing an unimpeded flow of technological change.

INTERDEPENDENCE AS A LEVER

Strategists can use the interdependence of technology as a lever for their strategy. One approach is to use a standout technology as a lever to raise the other technology elements to the same level. The logic of interdependence means that the various elements operate on the same level. The firm must live with the current level of technologies over the short term, but it can influence the future level of all its technologies. Unless all are brought up to the level of the strongest one, having a standout technology is of no use. Two outcomes are possible: either the standout element will revert to the lower level or the other elements will catch up to it; one element cannot stand out for long. Reversion to the lower level is more likely; in Japanese, there is an expression for it: "The nail that sticks out gets pounded down." Strategists must find a way to keep this from happening. If the other elements can be raised, then the drive for technical development will accelerate.

A good example is Matsushita's development of 8-millimeter video. The goal was to make the videotape recorder unit smaller and easier to carry. For the project to succeed, progress had to be made on several fronts: the tape, the deck, the magnetic recording and playback heads, parts, and assembly technology. When these areas were all at the necessary level of development, 8-millimeter video could become a reality. Figure 5–4 illustrates Matsushita's problem. The company decided to use its tape technology to drive development. They concentrated on a kind of tape they labeled a "dream tape," made by a metal vacuum evaporation process. This tape is much higher in quality than the conventional metal powder tapes but is harder to play and wears the head more quickly. Because Matsushita had already done a lot of work on this tape, it had a head start against the competition. The head of research and development at Matsushita, Shigeru Hayakawa, put it to me this way:

We wanted to force the rest of the technologies to a high level, and by developing this vacuum evaporation tape, with its superior quality to conventional tape, we hoped to do that. These other elements had to be of very high quality to mesh with the new tape. We had been working hard to improve those complementary video hardware technologies, but just mouthing a slogan like "work hard" by itself is sometimes not enough to achieve rapid progress. Vacuum evaporation tape played the role of the technology leader and helped us to achieve the progress we wanted. The improved hardware technology, in turn, has been used in our conventional videotape recorder deck and in the parts for that deck. The net result has been upgraded technology in all aspects of our videotape recorder technology. (Hayakawa, 1982)

The revolutionary tape technology put pressure on the engineering staff in charge of hardware to accelerate their development and gave them a specific target. They knew that the vacuum evaporation tape would have no value unless they did their part. Because technology elements are interdependent, a standout technology can put pressure on the whole organization to achieve a higher level of technology.

The mutual interdependence of technology is like a jigsaw puzzle. If one piece is changed, the whole puzzle may change. If one element in technology changes, a whole different picture may emerge. As a result, a firm may hesitate to make changes. Technology, especially in a mature

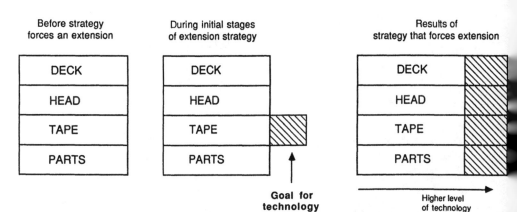

Figure 5–4. Stages in the development of Matsushita's video technology

stage, tends to become fixed, and this can block further progress. The vacuum tube and Swiss watch industries are good examples. No one wanted to rock the boat by introducing a new element. The new technology thus came from firms outside this industry, and in the end the firms still had to change.

To insure against the tendency toward stalemate in the firm's technology portfolio, the strategist can use technological interdependence to upset fixed relationships. Existing elements can be aggressively changed or new, heterogeneous elements introduced. This will create a new set of relationships and eliminate complacency. The system will have to find ways to coexist with the new elements and discover how to integrate the changes with the existing technology.

A new combination of elements has two advantages: it combines different sets of knowledge, and it brings together people with different ways of thinking. When seemingly unrelated elements are forced to coexist, entirely new technologies become possible. The production of man-made suede resulted from the merger of ultrafine textile technology and special processing technology. Existing optical technology coupled with new electronics technology made the automatic camera possible. New ceramic technology and existing engine technology are the basis for the ceramic engine.

Until the shape of the new technology becomes clear, the firm has to struggle with the transition. It has to deal with seemingly incompatible elements and with people who espouse different views. Conflicts are inevitable. As people acquire a specialty, they develop a characteristic way of thinking. An electrical engineer thinks differently from a mechanical engineer or a person who has always worked in the purchasing department. If top management puts people with different opinions together, the initial result will be confusion and suspicion. People tend to reject ideas they do not understand well. One will say, "He is really not very smart; he can't see the obvious answer to this problem." But these differing ways of thinking need not be counterproductive. The strategist can use that tension as a springboard. If these people have to remain in close contact with each other, they will begin to exchange ideas, which will eventually flower into new technology logics. Of course, a strategist must choose project members carefully to include different perspectives. And on a higher level, she must choose the portfolio of operations mission elements and of technology elements so that she is always introducing some new elements that are at odds with the established order.

For example, IBM showed its commitment to the Japanese market early by setting up a research facility in Japan in the 1950s. This operations mission decision turned out to have a dynamic effect, not just for Japan but for IBM's global strategy. Because Chinese character recognition was important in the Japanese software market, IBM's research labs worked hard to develop products with sophisticated scanning capabilities. Later, when advances in semiconductor technology made robotics feasible, this scanning ability enabled IBM computers to recognize the shapes of objects as well, and IBM was able to react quickly to this new market as well (Yamasaki and Takeda, 1976).

Technological fit as discussed in this chapter has many similarities to human nutrition. Without certain level of nutrition, an individual cannot live; only after this level is reached can the excess be directed toward building muscles and a strong body, accumulating for the future. However, excessive accumulation can lead to obesity. This applies as well to technology. After all, a firm accumulates technology and other assets to satisfy customer desires and thus make profits. Technology is only a means to reach these goals. A firm that goes overboard on accumulating technology may find that it has developed products that are five years ahead of their time or are too expensive to commercialize. There is an appropriate amount of technology accumulation: too little will starve the firm, but too much may suffocate it.

Kenjiro Takayanagi of Japan Victor, who pioneered the technology for the videotape recorder and the video disk, had this to say on the importance of a long-term objective for technological development:

> It takes at least ten years, usually twenty, to take a new idea through all the stages of research and development. To succeed, you have to have an organizational climate that supports such a long-term approach. You have to nurture and encourage researchers to apply themselves without an immediate payoff. Often young researchers want to be recognized within the company and by society. As a result, they want to take on research on "in" topics being worked on by other companies. Unfortunately, such atti-

tudes do not help the company foster original research ideas. We have to teach them to develop a long-term perspective, steadily bringing the important research themes to fruition. (Takayanagi, 1980)

A firm should never try to be in fit with technology for its own sake. Technological fit has meaning only in the context of strategies for customer fit and competitive fit. To find the appropriate level of technological fit, the strategist must try to anticipate changes in technology and in the firm.

Resource Fit

Up to this point I have discussed the external factors (customers, competition, and technology) with which strategy must fit. In the next two chapters I present the internal factors—corporate resources and the organization—necessary for fit. This chapter will consider the issues underlying effective utilization and efficient accumulation of resources and strategies for achieving these goals. In each case I will discuss not only static, one-period resource fit but also ways to keep resource fit over time.

Why discuss internal factors, when it is obvious that a firm lives or dies on its ability to effectively and continuously match its external environment? The answer is that to match the external environment, a firm must have good internal fit. Strategy is the linchpin that connects the internal and external factors and finds the most desirable shape for these interrelationships. Strategy must look both outward to the environment and inward to the firm itself through resource fit and organizational fit.

To effectively fit the environment, a person must live within his physical and psychological limits. At a minimum, he must set his existing limits to a level appropriate for the environment. The city dweller who goes to live in the Arctic must be sure he is in good physical and mental condition; he must adapt to different eating habits and must toughen himself for the stress of long periods of darkness. The situation is similar for a firm trying to match its internal factors to the environment. The company's resource levels and organizational climate limit its adaptiveness, much as a person's physical and mental limits restrict his ability to fit the environment.

Strategy and Existing Resources

A firm's strategy is made up of the current and future elements in its product/market portfolio, its operations mission, and its corporate resource portfolio. Resource fit can be approached in two ways. One way is for the strategist to look for preferred relationships between resources and strategy. From this perspective there are three key questions: Does the firm have sufficient *resource backing* to carry out its strategy? Does the firm's current strategy *effectively utilize* its current resources? Is the firm *efficiently accumulating* resources for the future?

The other approach is to focus on relationships within the strategy elements, evaluating various mixes of these elements to find the mix that effectively uses and efficiently accumulates corporate resources. Some mixes will improve performance, and others will not. The appropriate mix of strategy elements produces what I call a *combinatorial benefit*. Figure 6–1 shows the relationships to be examined in this chapter.

BACKING STRATEGY WITH SUFFICIENT RESOURCES

Good strategy is often said to capitalize on a company's strengths and to conceal its weaknesses, which is certainly true. This statement becomes more meaningful if one thinks about the relationships between current resources and strategy. Before a firm can decide how to accumulate and use its corporate resources, it must ascertain whether it has the resources to carry out a given strategy. Surprisingly, many companies undertake a strategy without realizing that they lack the necessary resources. During World War II the Japanese army at one time decided that it did not have to carry many supplies to carry out a campaign in Burma, since it would be capturing supplies as it went along. This strategy failed dismally, wasting thousands of lives.

There seem to be three reasons for firms choosing a strategy without having sufficient resources to carry it out: lack of careful analysis, difficulty in predicting future needs, and overestimation of current resources.

In the first case, those who designed the strategy may simply not have thought it through carefully. Strategy in this case becomes just a slogan. A more serious variation of this carelessness is shown when managers are unduly optimistic about the level of resources necessary to carry out the strategy.

A second blind spot is forecast error. If it is hard to project the required resources, mistakes may be made as the environment changes. Even a careful and conscientious manager may end up with insufficient backing for a strategy. Even if sufficient resources become available, they may not be accumulated in time to support the strategy. Forecasting is not easy. The strategist may be able to come close most of the time in deciding on the personnel, financial resources, and production facilities necessary for a given strategy, but that may not be enough. Invisible assets are often the most important resource for a successful strategy, and they are difficult to forecast. Such invisible assets as sen-

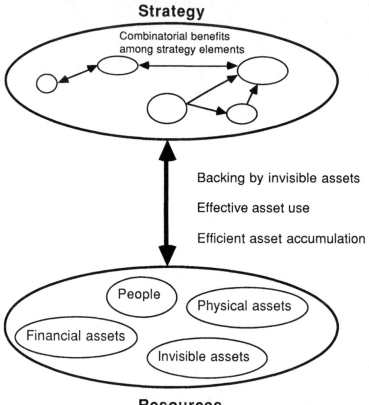

Figure 6–1. An overview of resource fit

sitivity to fashion may make or break a firm in the apparel industry; cosmetics success may be based on the ability to project a particular image. Each of these invisible assets has to be identified and its necessary level forecast. The greater the changes in the competitive environment, the more difficult this forecasting becomes.

An example will make the point. As the electronic calculator moved from the growth stage, in which it was a new and relatively expensive product, to the mature stage, in which it could be bought at the local drug store, companies were forced to develop various products from the basic one. The companies had to change to mass production, find ways to market the output, and develop production equipment that would handle a wide variety of products. Sharp and Casio were among the few firms that prepared the necessary resources to carry out their strategies.

Aida Engineering, a Japanese machinery company, illustrates how a company can define its product correctly and be prepared with the resources to meet key customer demands. Keinosuke Aida, the president of the firm, put it this way:

> Our company started out making machines, but we never thought of machines as mere chunks of metal, but rather as a tool for firms to use for efficient production. We even chose as our name, Aida Engineering, a name that stressed the provision of the software necessary to make the chunks of metal work for our customers. That is where we make our profits. Engineering implies we have the tools for problem solving. Customers do not come to us for a new machine unless they are facing some type of problem that they cannot solve with their current equipment. The firm might want to find ways to increase product quality or to do small lot production of a variety of products on an automated line. They know what they want their tools to do. We sell that performance through our lines of machinery. (Industrial Bank of Japan, 1979)

Aida Engineering had to do more than build machinery well. It realized that its key corporate resource was its ability to build systems that matched customer desires. Aida built and maintained its competitive position by consulting with clients and solving their problems.

The third reason for firms failing to prepare sufficient resource backing is that they misread their level of resources, especially invisible assets. Even if the strategist correctly calculates the level of resources *necessary* for a strategy, it may fail if the present level of resources has been misjudged. It is not difficult to find examples. When a Japanese sewing machine company decided to add consumer electronics to the products it sold door-to-door, it miscalculated the resources available for selling two completely different lines of products. At first the salespeople put more effort into selling the new electronics product line, since that seemed easier to sell. Sales of sewing machines dropped. But the salespeople were not able to sell the electronic appliances well, since they had insufficient knowledge and were not able to provide adequate service after the sale. As a result, the company lost its top ranking in sales of sewing machines and failed in its diversification moves.

This mistake is often made by American firms trying to enter the Japanese market. They assume that their invisible assets of worldwide reputation and well-known technology will be sufficient to enter the market. Safeway's initial attempt to develop an American-style supermarket in Tokyo without adjusting for higher land costs reflects their overestimation of the brand name's value. Procter and Gamble's initial attempt to sell detergent in Japan using exactly the same methods as in the United States also failed because they misread the competitive power of their internationally proven marketing assets.

UTILIZING RESOURCES EFFECTIVELY

A strategist might think that the firm should pile up enough resources to be absolutely sure that the backing is sufficient. The cost of that kind of safety is too high, however. As the old Japanese proverb says, "Too much is just like too little," because the firm cannot use those resources to gain some other strategic goal.

Even with sufficient backing for a strategy, some firms fail because they do not effectively use their resources to build successful strategies. A firm's resources are effectively utilized if none are idle, as long as the technology to apply them is available, and if the full potential of each resource is tapped. Every company must check for idle resources. If a plant is typically shut down during the winter, the company should consider developing a new product that would use the plant in that slack period. Not all idle resources are so easy to spot, however, and the firm has to pay special attention to identifying them. For example, a transport firm may not realize that its truck is running empty over some portions of the route. Once it spots this idle resource, it can look for new products to fill the empty slot.

Much harder than achieving full utilization, however, is taking full advantage of each resource. It is especially difficult to find the potential, and choose strategies to take advantage of the most important set of resources, invisible assets. Managers often agonize over such questions. "What's the technical potential of my firm?" "How much can we push through our distribution channel without straining its capacity?" If a company misreads the potential of its current resources, a strategy designed to utilize that potential will have insufficient resource backing. The sewing machine company's attempt at diversification illustrates this point. By misjudging the potential of its distribution capability and by not adjusting to this problem, the strategy was doomed to failure.

Some firms solve these problems smoothly. Both Casio and Sharp correctly read the potential of their invisible assets in integrated circuit technology, which they had nurtured with electronic calculators and similar products. Using this technology, Sharp successfully developed electronic home appliances and office information systems and Casio developed digital watches and electronic musical instruments.

In the 1950s several Japanese textile trading companies (for example, C. Itoh, Marubeni) that had developed sophisticated international trading systems found that some of their international resources (market information, shipping capacity, overseas offices) could be more fully utilized. By having an office in the United States, they could gather market information and handle other products. They predicted that customers who were unfamiliar with most Japanese companies would know their names and might rely on them to help market other products. These companies developed a wider portfolio of products and in the process became general trading companies.

ACCUMULATING RESOURCES EFFICIENTLY

Effective utilization of invisible assets implies that the firm must work only with the resources it currently possesses. It is easy to get caught up in this and be trapped into wrongly assuming that resources cannot be changed. But resources *do* change, and strategy is often the source of that change. When firms use their resources effectively, they create new invisible assets. Resource fit thus requires more than effective utilization of existing resources; efficient accumulation of new resources is just as important. New resources must be accumulated at *low cost, quickly, and in a timely manner.* It may be idealistic to try to achieve all three conditions at once, but each contributes to the ideal of efficient resource accumulation.

A system that efficiently accumulates resources usually shows one of the following patterns: either new resources are created as a by-product of a one-period strategy or resources developed in one strategy element are consciously used for the next element.

When new resources are a strategy by-product, they can be accumulated at low cost. Examples were presented in Chapter 2 in the discussion of invisible asset accumulation. To use resources developed in carrying out one strategy in other strategic areas—the second pattern—the supply of resources and the demand for them within the firm must be effectively matched, both in magnitude and in timing. When the profits generated from mature products are used to develop new products, the resources of one area of the firm are the base for the firm's entry into new product lines.

COMBINATORIAL BENEFITS

When resources and strategy fit well together, there are combinatorial benefits in both resource utilization and asset accumulation. The right combination of product/market segments or elements of the firm's operations mission in a strategy produces various benefits relating to the firm's resources. If a firm can use a single resource (say a plant, or some technology or skill) in more than one product/market segment, there is a combinatorial benefit from the two segments. Resources developed for one product can often reduce the required accumulation of resources for another product, either at the same time or in the future. Similarly, a combinatorial benefit results when operations in one area develop resources that can be used in other areas of the firm.

When a firm sells several types of products, another kind of combinatorial benefit occurs. Consumer confidence in the firm and the appeal of the product line increase. Panasonic, with its full line of electronics products, relies on its well-recognized brand name to sell a greater variety of products than Sony, which has a narrower product line. Recognizing the importance of this kind of diversity, Sony has established a series of stores that sell foreign brand-name electrical products. This enables Sony to get more benefit from its market reputation, a key invisible asset. A department store that stocks a wide range of products or an electronics manufacturer that provides a full line of products is realizing this type of combinatorial benefit, building up the invisible asset of consumer confidence.

A firm can combine strategy elements in many different ways: in products, in markets, in elements in the operations mission, or in current and future strategies. Figure 6–2 illustrates these relationships.

A combination of several strategy elements at one time uses a firm's assets more effectively. A combination of two strategies at two different times enables the firm to more efficiently accumulate invisible assets for the future. In other words, effective utilization of resources springs from static combinatorial benefits; efficient accumulation, from dynamic combinatorial benefits.

Efficient accumulation is closely connected to the dynamic combi-

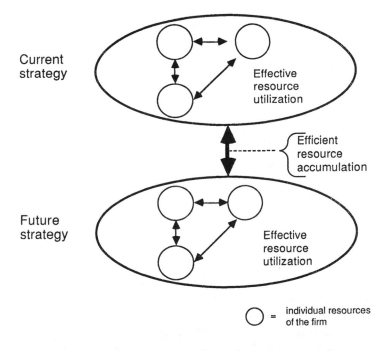

Figure 6–2. Combinatorial benefits and resource fit

natorial effect between current and future strategy for two reasons. First, it takes time to accumulate resources. If a current strategy leads to efficient accumulation, those resources have value only as the basis for later utilization. The Sony success (both in brand name and in technology) in transistor radios was the base for later success in television and other areas. Experience in selling textiles in developing countries gave Japanese trading companies knowledge about political and economic situations and the market information necessary for developing more complex deals such as industrial equipment contracts. Resource accumulation is inescapably tied to current and future strategy.

Current strategy has many spillover effects that affect future strategy as well. If current strategy generates cash flow or market information, for instance, these resources will affect the firm's future strategy. Braun, the German electronics firm, has had its own subsidiary to sell shavers in Japan since 1968. Hans Pauli, the president of the subsidiary, said, about the benefits of the office for global strategy formulation, "Certainly we are also a listening post for a European organization about what is going on in Japan, because this is the market from which the competition is coming. Japan has five or six major electrical appliance manufacturers, all of them producing electric shavers. They are competing against each other very heavily and in the process competing against us, too. They are also looking more toward Europe and the United States, so developments here have a big impact on what is going to happen elsewhere" (Murray, 1984).

Portfolio Effects

Combinatorial benefits result from a portfolio of strategy elements utilizing and accumulating resources effectively and efficiently. I will consider two types of portfolio effects: the complement effect and the synergy effect. Since the differences between the two types have not yet been made clear, an example will help. The manager of a ski resort hotel whose market is primarily skiers must be concerned about the seasonal nature of the business. Off season the facilities are idle. To deal with this problem the resort might build golf and tennis facilities to attract summer resort guests. By so doing it creates a combinatorial benefit between the winter ski market and the resort market, providing for stable profits throughout the year. Even if neither group by itself can generate enough revenue, the two groups together can be profitable. The firm's physical resource, its hotel, is effectively used.

This portfolio effect has two important characteristics. First, both markets use the same resource. Each market fills a void left by the other, putting excess resources to work. But there may be no further interaction between the two markets. In this sense they are complements. Improvement in one market will have no effect on the other market; if ski traffic increases, it will not affect summer resort occupancy.

But the combinatorial benefit of the two sets of hotel visitors may not be limited to the complement effect. If skiers find that the hotel is a good place to stay, some may return in the summer. And summer guests may decide to try the ski resort next winter. One market is able to ride free on the invisible asset (the hotel's reputation) developed by the other. Sales in one market (skiers) are no longer independent of those in the other (summer guests). The effect may be positive or negative, but it is very different from the complement effect discussed above. It is multiplicative rather than additive; this is synergy.

Previous studies have defined synergy as merely the whole portfolio effect, but I use the term in a narrower sense that is more in keeping with its original meaning. This requires the use of an additional term (complement effect), but the discussion in terms of these two types of portfolio effects enables us to dig more deeply into the portfolio effect. The synergy effect is one strategic level above the complement effect. With synergy something new is created, whose effects are more significant and wide-ranging than those of just full utilization. It obviously takes more than adding markets to achieve this result.

Compared to the complement effect, the synergy effect is difficult to achieve, and the strategist must make a greater effort to capture these benefits. A careless company might never be aware that they exist. Yet the difference between two companies in resource fit may be in the ability of one to ferret out synergy effects.

COMPLEMENT EFFECT

The complement effect almost always focuses on full capacity utilization of some kind. Just as the ski resort becomes a summer hotel, some Japanese auto carriers are filled with logs for the return voyage to Japan from the west coast of the United States. A personal computer manufacturer gets full use from the cash flow generated by an established model when it uses those funds to develop the next generation of models. Of course a complement effect can work with several products; the objective is always to combine elements so that resources are fully used.

Unless a firm has more than one product or market, its resources may not be used to capacity, resulting in lower sales or profits. Permitting two unrelated strategy elements to coexist, usually through the utilization of the same physical or financial assets, is the essence of the complement effect.

The most easily observable and perhaps most widespread complement effect is the use of the same physical asset to serve more than one market. A single product market might not be sufficient because optimal resource capacity does not match the size of the market, or because resources are not used with equal intensity over time, or because the required resource capacity fluctuates.

In the first case there is a gap between the logically optimal size of the firm's resource commitment and the volume of the operation in a single market. For example, it may not be possible to build a plant with just the right capacity to manufacture a single product; the gap can be filled by adding a second product. A good example is General Motors' auto engine plants. If an automobile division cannot use all of their capacity, GM permits the engine plants to build engines for its other divisions. Falling sales of one product may provide an opportunity to use part of the plant to produce another product.

Another opportunity to produce a complement effect arises when facilities are not used with equal intensity over a cycle, daily or seasonal. We have seen that in the hotel case, but a restaurant that serves an after-theater meal or a Sunday brunch is doing the same thing.

A third type of complement effect can be obtained when the level of physical resources necessary to operate in a given market fluctuates. A firm with several markets or products can be more confident that the total level of required resources will remain relatively stable. Each market has sales variability, but by operating in several, the firm reduces the total variability. Again, the GM engine plant is a good example. GM is able to forecast its overall sales better than sales of individual models. Having the flexibility to occasionally supply Chevrolet engines to other divisions helps GM maintain full operation of its engine plants. To take another example, as the domestic economies of Japan and the United States experience more variation, more and more firms are trying to enter export markets. Any firm can find potential areas for complement effect benefits if it pays attention to the problem.

The three conditions described for the complement effect for physical assets also apply to financial resources, but with a significant difference: financial resources are both an input and an output; they are *generated by* and *utilized in* business activities. This special characteristic will require some adjustments in the analysis. The first condition, underutilization of the resource, here means that funds generated by one product or market cannot be effectively recycled in that area. This idle money has to be funneled into other products or markets. Few companies are in that enviable position, but it is an important complement effect to keep in mind.

The second condition, inability to use a resource with the same intensity over a cycle, also applies to money, but the cycle is of longer duration because of the input/output nature of this resource. If the financial resources input in a product line do not match the cash flow generated, the potential exists for the second type of financial complement effect. A company that has a strong cash flow can use this resource to expand into new markets. The reverse situation can also exist. A computer leasing company frequently must search for short-term financing. One U.S. firm bought an insurance company to have access to current funds.

The imbalance between inflow and outflow may be in short-term or long-term funds or it may be seasonal, but it may also be between products at different life cycle stages. During the product development period funds are poured into the product line. In the growth period, more money flows in as investment in production and product development increases. When the product reaches the mature stage, however, little investment is needed, and money flows out. A firm that is conscious of this dynamic imbalance of cash inflow and outflow can design a multiproduct strategy to achieve a complement effect.

The third condition for complement effects, uncertainty about the future use of resources, also applies to the flow of financial resources. Thus firms choose to operate in several market segments to make balanced cash flows more likely. A firm that successfully deals with uncertainty in the use of its physical assets will create the potential for complement effects with its financial resources.

SYNERGY

The goal of synergy is to get a free ride. This happens when the resources accumulated in one part of the company are used simultaneously and at no additional expense by other parts. Ajinomoto, the Japanese condiments company, had developed a strong brand image and distribution network. It used those resources to sell other food products, such as salad oil, mayonnaise, and boullion cubes, and become a more diversified manufacturer. In addition, it used the amino acid technology developed for its condiments in a new pharmaceutical products division.

The potential for free rides is just as important in marketing as in production. Supermarkets advertise loss leaders to draw customers into stores, where they will also buy products with a higher mark-up. What they lose on these loss leaders is offset by the profits from the sales of other goods. Loss leaders and high-markup goods have to be present together to create synergy.

Sometimes two areas work together to take advantage of each other's strengths. In the hotel example the two market areas, ski customers and resort customers, take a free ride on the invisible assets such as the hotel's reputation, but the result is more than the sum of the two markets when they are put together.

Most physical resources do not offer the potential for a free ride or simultaneous usage. When two distinct areas of a plant are used to produce two different products, no synergy is created. Financial resources cannot be used simultaneously in two segments either. If money is poured into development of one product, less is available for other products.

Invisible assets are different. Unlike physical and financial resources, an invisible asset like technology can be used in more than one area simultaneously without reducing its value in other areas. When the Ajinomoto amino acid technology is used in a pharmaceutical product, it can still be used to develop products in other areas. This is a true free-ride situation. Not only do invisible assets hold their value with simultaneous multiple use, in some cases their value is enhanced. The invisible asset of the ski lodge's reputation may increase in value as more customers take advantage of the facility and its summer reputation spreads. Synergy results when several areas are free to use the resources without taking anything away from other parts of the firm.

The complement effect is created by utilizing visible assets; the synergy effect, by utilizing invisible assets.

The essence of invisible assets is information, and it is this characteristic, which is not shared by other resources, that makes a free ride possible. Only information-based assets can be used in multiple ways at the same time. Information has three characteristics that make synergy possible: it can be used simultaneously, it does not wear out from overuse, and bits of it can be combined to yield even more information.

For example, if one of the firm's technical people knows a lot about a particular process, she can pass along that knowledge to colleagues in another department. She can still use it herself, and it is available for others within the firm to use. In fact, this technology may increase in value as people share the results of their research. One department may know of a development that will enable them to combine two pieces of information to create additional valuable technology. Eventually the value of the information to other areas may lessen as it is dispersed, but the value of the information itself will not decline.

Synergy from information-based assets often enables a company to create a competitive edge. This can happen as the firm operates in new products and markets or as it chooses new strategies in established markets. A company that can call on the synergy from invisible assets such as product name or distribution channel control will have a competitive edge over a company without such assets. Ajinomoto, with its invisible assets in condiments marketing and production, was able to enter the mayonnaise market successfully when other companies failed. The synergy from invisible assets enables the firm to build a competitive position at lower cost. Of course good product design and careful implementation of strategy are important, but the basis of the success is synergy.

The complement effect also has potential for forging a competitive edge, but it is much more limited. Using an idle plant for a new product saves capital equipment costs and reduces the time needed to enter a new market, but these benefits stop when the new production line starts up and the plant is producing at full capacity. The limits on physical resources set the limits on the contribution of the complement effect. Financial resources are similarly limited. The benefits of a cash flow balance may be negated if competitors also have access to extra financial resources. This asset may not give the firm the competitive edge it is seeking.

With invisible assets, on the other hand, the competitive benefits from synergy can be both continuous and substantial. In Chapter 2 I stressed that invisible assets cannot be purchased but must be created within the firm over the long term. These assets give the firm a strong advantage over new competitors, who will need considerable time to create similar resources. With effective use of synergy, the strategist can make even better use of this competitive advantage. By taking a free ride on the synergy inherent in invisible assets, the firm can create very effective and long-lasting competitive weapons.

The potential for achieving resource fit is reduced substantially if synergy benefits are not considered. Thus, a strategist has to keep invisible assets constantly in mind by asking questions like the following. "What kind of invisible assets does this product or market create?" "Can the assets be used in other areas of the firm?" "Am I making the best possible use of the invisible assets I have?" "Is this strategy limited to the complement effect benefits?" "Am I falling into the trap of being satisfied with just the complement effect?"

A strategy based on synergy can fail for various reasons, including the following: overestimating the benefits of synergy, assuming that all joint uses generate synergy, and developing too many unprofitable "synergy-creating" products. A company that overestimates the synergy benefits will find that the effect is much smaller than it anticipated, and the strategy may fail. Because it is difficult to estimate synergy benefits, it is best to be conservative in projections.

A second pitfall is to assume that *any* joint use of invisible assets will benefit the firm. The Nikon case shows the danger here. In marketing the Nikon EM, a less expensive, mass-produced camera, Nikon was able to take a free ride on its high-quality brand image, the Nikon mystique. But there was a risk that the Nikon EM might damage Nikon's reputation for superior quality. A firm must be aware of the potential for damaging its invisible asset base and try to anticipate any potential negative repercussions.

There is yet a third pitfall. A product may contribute to a firm's overall portfolio, even if it is not profitable. There may be a temptation to justify an unprofitable product by suggesting that it will enable other products to take a free ride. Any such suggestion should be examined carefully to ensure that it is justified.

Even though the payoff is higher for synergy, a strategist might argue that the return from complement effects is still important for competitive edge. After all, it is easier to keep track of physical assets than invisible assets. An idle plant is easily noticed; if money is available, people will want to make use of it. Taking advantage of the complement effect is certain to pay off. Unfortunately, this is one reason that the competitive benefits from the complement effect are not long-lasting: all the competitors are doing it. It pays to seek out synergy effects, for they will be longer-lasting and harder to duplicate.

In fact, a firm may not have to choose between complement and synergy effects because in many cases they can be pursued simultaneously. Potential complement and synergy benefits are often closely related, as the hotel example showed. Still, many companies, satisfied with the complement effect, tend to miss opportunities to take full advantage of the synergy potential within their firm. The cost of this oversight is high.

Dynamic Resource Fit

Over time, a company's accumulation of resources changes, and as a result its strategy must change. A company must recognize the dynamic nature of both its environment and of its resources. Dynamic combinatorial benefits result from combining present and future strategies; the two must mesh well to achieve this effect. Effective strategy in the present builds invisible assets, and the expanded stock enables the firm to plan its future strategy, bridging the gap between present and future strategy. A current strategy has to create enough resources for future strategy to be carried out. And the future strategy must make effective use of the resources that have been amassed. With these two steps, a firm has the dynamic combinatorial effect, which is the basis of dynamic resource fit.

A static combinatorial effect comes from the combination of different strategy elements at the same time. The dynamic combinatorial benefit, in contrast, is based on the combination of two strategies at different points in time. This is a very different type of portfolio effect.

Current resource accumulation strategy has to satisfy both present and future strategic requirements. When a company chooses a strategy, it is in fact making certain changes in its invisible asset portfolio for the future. A company that decides to advance into a new operation and makes the appropriate investment in plant, equipment, and research and development, with the necessary financing, has changed the set of resources available for use in the future. The future stock of resources is thus set by current policy.

Resources may also be accumulated as a by-product of current strategies in the product/market portfolio and the operations mission. In this way both financial resources and invisible assets are created without any direct effort by the firm. Matsushita's overseas strategy for batteries, discussed in Chapter 2, is an example of this route. The company created invisible assets in knowledge of the market, trained workers, and skills developed through producing and distributing simple batteries. These assets then became sources of dynamic synergy. Invisible assets and financial resources can be accumulated via both routes, but physical assets can be accumulated only through the first.

The future stock of resources is the variable that connects present and future strategies. Dynamic resource fit thus is, in essence, the creation of the most effective combinatorial benefit of these two strategies. The firm has to decide what current strategy is necessary to obtain this effect, and then how to frame its future strategy to capitalize on the effect. If the current and future strategies mesh well, they create either a dynamic complement effect or a dynamic synergy effect, or both. The effects are essentially the same as in the static case.

DYNAMIC COMPLEMENT EFFECT

The two key points for realizing the dynamic complement effect from physical resources are using resources effectively over time and securing the appropriate level of resources for strategy at each point in time. The complement effect depends on current and future strategies sharing the same assets or on current resources being reused for future strategy goals. Reusable physical assets are strategically valuable, and a firm should try to accumulate such resources.

For example, if a firm must decide whether to build a specialized assembly line for some of its products, it could design the plant with the potential for changing over to production of another product. This may make it much less efficient, however. In that case it may be better to design the assembly line so that it can be easily scrapped when it becomes outmoded, and to create a corporate culture that accepts change when a scrapping decision has to be made.

The important point about dynamic resource fit is that resource inputs and outputs must match. Cash flow is one measure of that matching, since it compares the total financial resources for all operations (the money outputs) with the cash expenditures for reinvestment within the firm (the money as an input). If financial resources are to be balanced in a dynamic sense, the strategist must consider not just where the flow of resources will come from within established operations, but also what financial resources the firm's divisions will require. For example, if a firm undertakes several operations with potential growth simultaneously, the strategist must be aware that after two or three years each one will require more investment if growth is to continue. Present strategies must generate enough cash to support the expected growth later, or the strategist must be willing to accept outside financing.

The cash flow requirements of a given product or market segment vary according to the stage of the product's life cycle, the size and growth rate of the market, and the product's competitive edge. At any one time, a product may be either a net user or a net generator of cash flow.

At the early stages in its life cycle, the product is most likely to use cash flow. As the cycle progresses, it should generate cash flow. Without holding constant the other two factors, however, the exact pattern cannot be determined. A segment with a faster rate of growth will require a large investment over a short period, slowing the shift to cash flow generation. The third factor is competitive edge. Other things being equal, a firm with a strong competitive position can generate a given sales volume at lower cost because it has lower production costs, based on accumulated knowledge or large-scale facilities, or lower sales cost, based on an established brand image. To change that firm's position, a competitor would have to commit substantial resources.

To get the dynamic complement effects from cash flow, a firm must first choose products and markets with different current cash flows. The next step is to preserve that complementary pattern over time. Conventional wisdom says that the ideal balance of product or market segments is struck when all cash-draining elements with no future are purged from the portfolio, except for a few unprofitable but promising new areas where the cash flow from current successes can be used. Since many of the currently unprofitable but growing areas may have an uncertain future, some should be kept, just in case. This is the basic message of the now famous Product Portfolio Management (PPM) techniques. The purpose of this method is to create the dynamic complement effect of cash flow by systematically combining different products and selecting matching strategies.

DYNAMIC SYNERGY

There is always the potential for dynamic combinatorial benefits from synergy, with future strategies getting a free ride on the invisible assets generated by current strategy. If the future strategy can start before the current strategy has exhausted all potential use of the invisible asset, so much the better. Where the periods of use overlap, contemporaneous use of the resources creates a static synergy effect, too. This use of invisible assets over time is illustrated in Figure 6–3.

The Casio example presented in Chapter 2 is a good illustration of this effect. The company was able to take advantage of the semiconductor chip technology accumulated in its electronic calculator business to advance into digital watches. At present Casio is also getting the benefit of the static synergy effect shown in Figure 6–3, since currently both calculators and watches are reaping benefits from this semiconductor technology. Current strategy calls for using semiconductor chip technology to develop office automation equipment and electronic musical instruments.

As I emphasized in Chapter 2, invisible assets are accumulated through implementation of the firm's strategy in the operations route and through competitive pressures in the market. For example, Casio's semiconductor chip technology was a response to competition in electronic calculators. This produces the pattern shown in Figure 6–4.

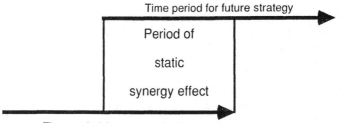

Figure 6–3. Dynamic synergy and static synergy

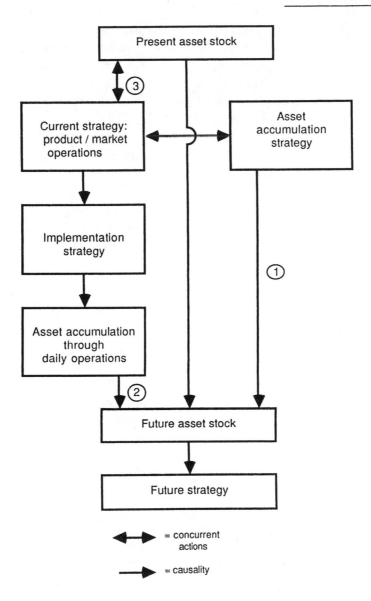

Figure 6–4. A basic framework for dynamic synergy

Ricoh's decision to reenter the camera market illustrates a strategy aimed at dynamic synergy. Ricoh was once a leading camera manufacturer in Japan; 65 percent of its sales in 1955 were in camera equipment. After a long period in which the company focused on the copy machine market, their camera market share was down to 3 percent in 1977. At that time Ricoh decided to reemphasize cameras. Ricoh's president, Takeshi Ohue, said, "The camera is Ricoh's only consumer product. Consumer goods are better at building brand image than capital goods. If Ricoh is to achieve the goal of becoming a multinational company, we have to build up our own brand image, and the camera is a good way to do that" (Michida, 1979). Because Ricoh had not exported its copy machines under its own name (Savin bought them to sell under its own name in the United States), the company's brand name was not established overseas. By building brand name recognition through camera sales, Ricoh has been able to take a free ride on that reputation for other products.

The key to corporate growth lies in generating this dynamic synergy. Whenever the strategies that have resulted in superior growth are analyzed, one finds this basic principle at work. Dynamic synergy is essential for two reasons. First, invisible assets can be effectively accumulated and used over a long period only by taking advantage of dynamic synergy giving firms the resources to actively adapt to the ever-changing environment. Second, dynamic synergy between two product or market segments makes it easy to create a dynamic complement effect for financial resources at the same time. As Figure 6–3 shows, when the life cycles of two products overlap, it is often possible to match the cash flow inputs and outputs. By aiming at dynamic synergy, dynamic complement effects often emerge naturally.

To generate dynamic synergy, a firm should choose activities that create invisible assets, design strategy with dynamic synergy in mind, and go beyond its current abilities to develop these invisible assets.

The choice of product or market portfolio elements or operations mission can influence the future level of invisible assets. The flow of invisible assets does not come automatically. If a firm selects product or market portfolio elements only on the basis of cash flow or return on investment, without considering resource accumulation, it will never reap this synergy benefit. Careless application of product portfolio management will often lead to this result.

Kirin Beer chose to further develop its market for nonalcoholic drinks by accepting Coca Cola's offer of a bottling franchise when the American company entered the Japanese market after World War II. Coca Cola's worldwide strategy was to choose firms with bottling expertise and strong financial positions as franchise bottlers rather than owning the facilities itself. At that time Kirin Beer did not have much experience in nonalcoholic drinks, but through its Coca Cola franchise, Kirin developed a better knowledge of the market and the production process. These invisible assets eventually enabled Kirin to enter the soft drink market and eat into Coca Cola's market share by catching the switch in Japanese tastes to fruit and juice drinks earlier than its partner.

Operations mission decisions can sometimes have a greater effect on the accumulation of invisible assets than product or market decisions. If a firm puts too much emphasis on the latter, it may neglect operations-based avenues to resource accumulation, as happens when a firm bases its entire strategy on marketing considerations.

My second point is that the strategy for dynamic synergy requires designing the flow of events, setting out the dynamic changes step by step and determining the timing and order of those changes. The flow of strategy cannot be designed by considering only a single period. Product and operations mission decisions at any one time have to be seen in light of the overall flow of strategy. Each step must be designed with the overall flow in mind, achieving dynamic equilibrium as well as development within the design.

Casio's flow of strategy succeeded because the digital watch came after the electronic calculator; the reverse would not have worked. This is true also of the company's entry into the electronic musical instrument market. In Matsushita's foreign plants, battery production as an end in itself would not have had much meaning. As part of the company's strategic design, however, it was a very significant first step. A firm that develops a strategic design will find the hidden benefits of dynamic synergy within it. Then the door to the next market will be easier to unlock, as Casio found.

A company that does not design a strategy to generate a positive flow of resources can find itself in a vicious circle. If present strategies fail to generate the resources necessary for future strategies, the firm will be forced to eat into its resource base, reducing its options for future strategic moves. Chronically troubled companies are often trapped in this type of pattern.

The dynamic aspect of strategic design leads to my third point: the necessity for *imbalance* at times. Less than adequate backing for a strategy may not always be damaging and can be quite beneficial over the long haul, leading to the realization of the overall strategic design. I call this strategy *overextension*. In the cycle of dynamic synergy, a current lack of resources forces a firm to generate new invisible assets that will assure the success of future strategy. It would be ideal if these invisible assets could be created without overextension, but that is seldom possible in the reality of the business world. To achieve its strategic design, a firm may have to enter a new product area or operations mission activity before it is completely ready. Something I often hear in talking with successful strategists sums up this point well: *"Overextend yourself, but don't get reckless."*

DYNAMIC IMBALANCE

Sometimes strategy must take a calculated risk. In Figure 6–4, short-term resource matching requires that current resources be sufficient for the strategies chosen. Overextension requires that the firm consciously violate the principle of static resource fit. This is not as contradictory as it sounds. Of course, some resource backing (physical resources, short-term capital) is essential for a strategy to be operative. Invisible assets, however, are important for effective strategy implementation so in the short term a strategy can make do with a little less than the necessary level of invisible assets. The short-term strategy may not be a winning one, but it may be worthwhile. Competition will toughen and train the people in the firm, and quite possibly some invisible assets will be acquired along the way.

Casio's semiconductor chip strategy illustrates the overextension strategy. Faced with fierce competition in the electronic calculator market, Casio had to jump into integrated circuit design to survive, even though it did not have the best technology in that area. That technology was forged in the heat of competition, eventually leading to Casio's current position in the market. Casio began with less than adequate resource backing, less than fully balanced resources. This short-term imbalance led to the creation of a solid base for future strategy that enabled Casio to beat back the competition in this market. This I call *dynamic imbalance*.

I do not advocate static resource imbalance for its own sake. I believe, however, that imbalance is usually beneficial, especially for invisible assets and for companies that are growing rapidly. The short-term imbalance works as an impetus to achieve dynamic resource fit. If resources are *not* matched in a static sense at key times in the life of the firm, this imbalance can be the basis for corporate growth and strategy.

The Japanese auto industry is a good illustration of the potential payoff from dynamic imbalance. In the early 1950s some Japanese thought that the industry did not have the resources necessary to be competitive internationally. Bank of Japan Governor Ichimada argued that Japan would have to compete on too large a scale and over too wide a range of market segments. He argued that the industry lacked the skills for international competition. Japan could not produce high-quality sheet steel for automobiles, and the domestic machine tool industry could not build the machines to grind the engine blocks. The Japanese automobile industry could not compete because it needed so many supporting industries, he thought. An imbalance existed between corporate resources, especially invisible assets, and the automobile production strategy. Proponents argued that the wide scope of supporting industries was an attraction. As the industry grew, they argued, the related industries would grow with it. These spillover effects could not be ignored. Producing cars would be the only way to eliminate the short-term imbalance gradually, and the accumulated resources would enable the firms to be competitive.

The proponents won the debate, and the Japanese auto industry was protected from international competition long enough to develop the needed resources. Of course it could not produce internationally competitive cars right away. The first Japanese cars tested on American roads could not stand the sustained speeds and failed miserably. This sort of situation is now in the past for cars and many other Japanese products, but the lesson is worth remembering. In each of these industries an overextension strategy was crucial to accumulating sufficient resources to become competitive in world markets. By creating a static imbalance between resources and operations (route 3 in Figure 6–4), the flow of additional resources for use in future strategy (route 2) is increased. There is no assurance that successive short-term imbalances will lead to the desired long-term balance. Still, avoiding all short-term imbalances means giving up the potential for dynamic synergy.

If there is potential for long-term balance through short-term imbalance, a strategist should not be content as the benefits from previous imbalances work through the system and the system settles down. Such a situation should be seen as a signal for new overextension initiatives for an even higher level of long-term balance through imbalance. This logic says: *destroy balance*.

Organizational Fit

Let's look at the differences between individual and corporate strategy. When an individual plans her own activities, she has only to decide on a strategy that she feels satisfied with. Because she has a good idea of what needs to be accomplished and how various outcomes will affect her, strategy development is relatively easy. The environment is well known and clearly defined, making it relatively easy to find strategies that fit it. Once set, the strategy need not be sold to anyone, so she can get right to work carrying it out.

In corporate strategy, however, the strategist must consider people other than herself at every phase. It is not the strategist but other people who carry out the strategy. Their efforts, each of them on a relatively small scale, will lead to success. It is the people in the sales force, the workers on the production line, the researchers on development teams who boost sales and generate profits. A manager will achieve her strategy goals only if all these people are willing to work to achieve them. For strategy to succeed, more is necessary than a superbly written plan or a brilliant strategist. If only the strategist knows and understands the plan, the organization will not move, it will go nowhere. Those who carry out the strategy must be able to use it as a guide in their day-to-day work. The people in the organization decide the organization's performance.

People in a firm have their own interests, their own patterns of thinking and feeling. They have knowledge and the capacity to learn. To mobilize people in their everyday activities, the strategist must take into consideration their interests, strengths, and weaknesses as well as the relationships among individuals. Various kinds of communication channels have been set up, and feelings of conflict, trust and comradeship are already in place. The organization as a whole also has a unique corporate culture built up over time.

A successful strategy has to deal with and influence all these factors in order to have organizational fit. Does the strategy match the characteristics of the people in the firm it is expected to influence? Is the strategy being effectively communicated to the members of the organization? These are the questions of organizational fit. But even that is not enough: a strategy must also provide a stimulus, something that transcends the employees' self-interest and individual ways of thinking.

Up to this point, the discussions of environmental and resource fit have been based on economic analysis, but the discussion of organizational fit includes something more. It requires careful analysis of the strengths and weaknesses of the people who will carry out the strategy and an understanding of the group dynamics of the organization. The logic is behavioral here.

Strategy and the Organization

It is often assumed that the only time a strategist has to worry about members of the organization is in implementing strategy, that only the people who implement the policy have to take the organization into account. To use the terms developed in this book, the common belief is that the strategists should consider only environmental and resource fit in deciding strategy and let the implementers make sure that the organization follows it.

This is a dangerous miscalculation. It makes no sense to ignore the effect strategy will have on the people in an organization. Nor does it make sense to ignore their probable reactions to a new policy. The content of strategy must be developed with the organization psychology in mind. Human aspects are too important to be left to implementation. Organizational fit must be developed along with environmental and resource fit.

It is not unusual for organizational fit to be the deciding factor in a corporation's decision about a new strategy initiative. Managers may decide against pursuing a particular strategy if it is obvious that it will never be accepted within the company. Or a firm may choose a strategy to improve organizational fit. Keizo Saji, president of Suntory, the largest whiskey manufacturer in Japan, explained why the company entered the beer market:

When we decided to get into the beer industry in 1963, I started with a feeling that our future in the whiskey market may not be that bright. The reaction I got was, "Our share in the whiskey market is high; why take the risk of crossing over to challenge this new market?" Somehow, I didn't think we could be so complacent. We could not just keep doing what we were doing. It was a lot different from the current conditions when we can hold our own with the foreign brands. At that time, Japanese whiskey was protected from the strong import competition in many ways. I thought that the company could not survive and prosper if it remained only in this whiskey industry. Getting into the beer business would certainly present problems, but we had to develop a field other than whiskey, and I also hoped this would stimulate the company, giving it new vitality. (*Toyo Keizai,* Aug. 27, 1983)

The decision to go after the beer market was made not just to achieve environmental or resource fit, though these incentives were clearly present. Saji was worried that his organization was getting soft; being the "whiskey king" in Japan was no longer a challenge. He hoped that entering the beer market would energize the company. It is generally agreed that this strategy has succeeded. The stimulus and hard work of getting into the beer market led to organizational changes that spilled over into the marketing of whiskey, thus improving the overall performance of the firm.

Two aspects of organizational fit need to be discussed. One is the effective communication of the chosen stategy to the organization. A strategy is most likely to lead to success if it is effectively communicated and promoted throughout the organization in ways that are consistent with the corporate culture. The other aspect is the choice of strategy content. The strategy content must fit the firm's psychological features and be able to mobilize the organization. This is the angle that Suntory focused on.

EXPLICITNESS
To lead the organization, a strategy must be clear to the people within it. This may seem obvious, but it is very important. A manager may have an excellent idea, but unless he is able to communicate it to his organization, it will never be carried out.

Why must a strategy be explicitly stated? Would it not be possible just to give each employee very specific instructions without explaining the overall strategy? In a firm that depends on the strong leadership of a single owner or manager, this may be possible. That person knows the blueprint for the firm, and the employees follow specific orders to put their individual pieces into place, not knowing how they will fit together.

But in most firms an explicit strategy is necessary for at least four reasons. First, if each of the operating activities takes the same direction, according to a clearly presented strategy, then the activities will naturally be coordinated. This should happen without additional direction from management. Construction workers do not have to ask what to do each time they run into a problem; they just look at the plans. With the basic direction established, the strategist can expect that the company's energies will be focused in a common direction.

The second reason for having an explicit strategy is to ensure that each operating activity is done according to the long-term view presented by the strategy. Without this explicit guidance, workers' actions will be based on their own short-term considerations, especially when they are pressed to complete their everyday work. Presenting a clear long-term strategy to each worker helps avoid this danger.

A third benefit of an explicit long-term strategy is that it gives people a dream, which can boost morale and help hold the organization together. Such a strategy lays out the future of the firm and gives basic guidance on how to reach that goal. When clearly presented, the goals become part of each individual's goals, and the employee begins to think of his future place in the organization. This can be a greater source of motivation than short-term financial incentives. A company beginning a large construction project will often put a model in the offices of those who are working on the project to show everyone the shape of the future building. This creates a sense of participation and a lever for motivation. Such a vision is an important result of a clear and explicit strategy.

The last reason for an explicit strategy is that it provides a shield against anxiety during times of change within the firm. The team that developed the IBM PC was certainly faced with anxiety. They were told to use outside sources and provide hardware details to outsiders, instructions that contradicted the company's conventional approach.

The project members were faced with strong competitors, something they had not had to deal with in previous IBM projects. IBM management lessened that anxiety by linking the potential success of the program to the company's strategy, namely, denying competitors in the specialty mainframe and minicomputer markets the opportunity to establish a market position.

The best bulwark against anxiety is the confidence of top management. If that confidence can be transferred down through the organization, it will become embedded there. In this sense the strategy helps not only the people in the organization but top management as well.

An explicit strategy also fosters a corporate culture that values a long-term view and planning. A clear presentation of basic strategy encourages *all* members of the organization to adopt that way of thinking. During times of rapid change, there is a temptation to undertake business activities without planning, just reacting to immediate conditions. In such an environment the benefits of an explicit strategy are especially important. Everyone's actions must be guided by that strategy if the firm is not to be overwhelmed by the changes. It is the only way the firm can go beyond merely reacting to changes to influence the future shape of the competitive environment. An organization with a long-term strategy will soon pull away competitively from one with a short-term reactive strategy.

If top management does not have an explicit strategy, subordinates will not acquire the habit of strategic thinking. The lack of an explicit strategy is most costly when changes must be made. Without planning, suggestions for change can be misinterpreted, since there is no overall strategy by which to evaluate them. Often these suggestions are interpreted as personal attacks on those in charge. In that case a lot of time is wasted developing a corporate response to the change; in fact, some organizations may not be able to respond to change at all.

If management does not have an explicit strategy, it is hard to decide whether a firm is successful. Without objective criteria, it is easy to ascribe the success to the personal qualities of the managers. A company may initially grow because of the strong leadership of a single person. When that firm faces a change in the environment and must make a change in strategy, it may be unable to react, and its fortunes may change. Often no one in the organization dares to propose any change to the president for fear that it will be taken as a personal attack on his leadership. Many people attribute the demise of Osborne Computers to the unwillingness of people in that organization to question the founder's personal judgment (Bellew, 1984).

PENETRATION

Though it is essential for strategy to permeate all parts of the organization, the process necessary to accomplish this is far from obvious. Penetration may be more difficult than formulation of a good strategy. A significant portion of failed strategies are the result not of incorrect formulation but of insufficient penetration of the strategy into the organization. A strategy that is appropriate analytically may fail if it does not reach everyone in the firm, because the actions of the organization as a whole are not focused in the direction required by the strategy. It is quite conceivable that a rather ordinary strategy could work much better than one with a brilliant analysis of environmental and resource fit. The difference would be in execution, if the lesser strategy were carried out thoroughly by the entire organization.

If strategy is ingrained throughout the organization, then top management can expect that each business activity will respond in unison. It is a bit like a variety of Japanese rolled sweets called *kintaro ame* that have the same face no matter where the roll is sliced. I am not saying that this way of thinking is a panacea, but many companies that have gone through the great amount of effort necessary to develop a common understanding of strategy have been quite successful.

For example, Amada, a machine tool manufacturer, has resurrected several failing companies. In commenting on what made these companies fail and what Amada did to rehabilitate them, the chief executive officer, Isamu Amada, said:

> A company fails because the policies of top management have not penetrated to the lower echelons of the organization. If the organization is not well coordinated at these lower levels, people can do things inconsistent with policy without being challenged. To rebuild such a company, you have to do some "brainwashing," if you will, even though that idea has a bad connotation. Amada had to make workers realize that the company was previously run too loosely. All this may look rather simple to do, but it is very hard to take a company like that and shape it into one that follows

Amada methods. Once our policy is well understood, the crisis, we think, is half over. (Amada, 1979)

Top management has the responsibility of ensuring that strategy penetrates the organization and is understood by all. The leaders can do this through various means: speeches and persuasion, symbolic actions, changes in the evaluation system, slogans that set pertinent goals, and use of charisma. Figure 7–1 presents the main points in each of the methods.

The first and most obvious way to make strategy permeate the organization is to repeatedly persuade *by words*. The leaders may have to explain the strategy to the organization any number of times, constantly stressing its importance. This may require seemingly endless meetings with different groups.

Although words are very effective, the leader should not neglect symbolic actions, which can also help the strategy penetrate the organization. A symbolic action shows the direction of strategy clearly at an early stage. Top management could announce a major restructuring of the organization, putting people with real power in key positions to carry out the strategy. When Kodak in the spring of 1984 began a drive to increase its market share in Japan, it created a new division for Japan alone, separating it from the division that covered Asia and Africa. In addition, it assigned a former head of its strategic planning unit, a man with a known reputation in the company, as the manager of the new division. This action made clear the importance to Kodak of the new Japan strategy (Treece, 1985). Visits by managers to those workplaces where key elements of strategy are being carried out can

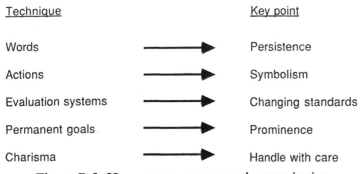

Technique		Key point
Words	⟶	Persistence
Actions	⟶	Symbolism
Evaluation systems	⟶	Changing standards
Permanent goals	⟶	Prominence
Charisma	⟶	Handle with care

Figure 7–1. How strategy penetrates the organization

help as well, as can meetings with outside people who are associated with the chosen direction. At this stage, the leader has to be a good actor.

Sometimes incentives can send a very strong message. Top management can use evaluation standards to encourage people to focus on areas that are essential to the overall strategy. Once this policy is in place, those who do not carry out their responsibilities in accordance with it will not receive a good evaluation. Employees who work against such a clear policy will obviously be given no credit.

Changes in evaluation standards tend to lag behind changes in strategy, especially when the firm must adjust to a rapidly changing environment. In such a situation an existing evaluation system can work against effective strategy. Suppose top management is working out a strategy to enter a new business, knowing that there will be some cost in short-term profits. If the firm retains the old evaluation system based on short-term profits, it will be hard to sell the new endeavor within the organization. A manager's natural reaction will be, "I understand what management wants, but as long as I am being evaluated under the old system, I see no reason to shift my efforts to this new area." To get workers to commit themselves to the new strategy, the evaluation standards should be adjusted. In certain cases the evaluation system may need a complete overhaul. Performance evaluation should be considered as a tool for making strategy permeate through the organization.

Sumitomo Bank was saddled with losses in the early 1970s when two of its major customers, the general trading company Ataka and the automaker Mazda, experienced serious financial crises. The bank, once the most profitable in Japan, dropped back. Ichiro Isoda, the president, realized that he had to keep company morale up during the crisis and at the same time look beyond it, setting the goal of again becoming the most profitable bank. "It was a matter of keeping up company morale. Once we got used to the idea that we would be just another middle-level bank, our people would never have the grit to try to get back to the top." Changing the evaluation system was important in reaching that goal. Previously Sumitomo Bank had been known for punishing managers for a single mistake, which Isoda felt gave the wrong signals in the changed situation. "Mr. Isoda felt this practice tended to cramp branch managers, to make them supercautious. They should be going out and cultivating new customers aggressively, he said. If one loan turned sour, this should not be held permanently against a line officer. 'It took two years for people to realize that I meant what I said,' commented Mr. Isoda, but the results were gratifying. Mr. Isoda said he could feel the whole bank's morale tightening up. People were on their toes" (Oka, 1982). The bank is again the most profitable in Japan.

Another way to have strategy permeate the organization is to use slogans to set pertinent goals. When employees carry out a strategy scenario, they want to know what the firm expects to accomplish and what conditions will result from a successful strategy. Strategy provides a scenario for company activities, showing the desirable image to be achieved. If the goal to be reached is presented to the organization along with the strategy, two positive effects can be expected. The first is increased acceptance. When people understand what the strategy is trying to do, they will be more commited to it. They will follow orders more willingly if they know why they are to take such actions.

Second, a goal can help people visualize the strategy and help them understand it. If the strategist announces a specific action but does not make the goal clear, people may interpret the action in a number of ways. This situation can lead to confusion. A large investment in plant and equipment is consistent with a drive to be best in cost efficiency, but it is also consistent with distribution into wider markets. The two strategies require rather different sets of actions; clearly presented goals will help the organization understand the purpose of the strategy.

For example, a financial institution that wants to expand internationally can set a goal of becoming internationally renowned. With this goal, it can proceed with specific actions, such as strengthening overseas branch networks and consolidating foreign and domestic operations. The strategist can feel confident that the people in the organization will realize that these strategy elements are related and have priority. If they understand the goals, members of the organization will make their own commitment to this strategy.

In one sense, since I have defined strategy as a scenario for achieving goals, they are the starting point for the strategic concept. But it is not always easy in practice to establish goals first, especially when they must be coupled with a strategy scenario. Without clear and specific goals, a strategy will lack a focus, and the organization will not be able to grasp the entire picture. Goals can provide just such a focus. Strategy does not work without a goal, and vice versa; both must be present for successful organizational fit.

Charisma is a final means by which the manager can make a strategy penetrate the organization. With charisma, top management can convince the employees that the plan is reasonable. People judge a presentation not just by what is said but by who is saying it. When the leaders are charismatic, people believe what they say and are more willing to follow them. Every leader should cultivate a certain degree of charisma.

A firm can become too dependent on charisma, however. If all the credit for a successful strategy is given to one top manager, the strategy becomes associated with that person, and any attack on it is then interpreted as a personal attack. This can lead to blind acquiescence to management's future policy decisions. A firm should be cautious in using charisma, which alone is not sufficient for making sure strategy permeates the organization.

Using Strategy to Mobilize People

In designing the content of strategy, the strategist must take into consideration the characteristics of the organization so that the chosen strategy will be able to mobilize people. Often strategy has to follow the organization rather than vice versa. In this respect there are three levels of organizational fit: providing a focus to unify the organization, creating momentum, and sustaining creative tension. For strategy to be effective, it should focus the organization's activities in the desired direction. A carefully planned strategy should provide a set of guidelines for everyone, a blueprint for all activities. This is the most basic sense in which a strategy must have organizational fit.

But organizational fit requires more than having everyone's actions focused in the same direction. People must feel commited to that direction; they must enthusiastically support that movement. As the organization gets used to moving in the right direction, *momentum* is created. This is the second level of organizational fit. If a firm does not have momentum, merely selecting the correct direction will not work well. The strategic push needs the latent power of this momentum. If organizations were mere machines, then this would not matter, but groups of people have this extra latent power that the strategist can tap.

The third level of organizational fit is creative tension. Even when a firm is heading in the right direction and has momentum, it may begin to feel self-satisfied and go slack. Because of this potential for slack, an organization needs some stimulus to remain in shape. Obviously, constant creative tension is not optimal. The strategist will have to decide on the level, type, and timing of tension. If used appropriately, creative tension can make the other elements of organizational fit more effective.

Each succeeding level of organizational fit builds on the base of the lower levels. Without a unifying focus, momentum will shunt the firm off in the wrong direction. Without momentum and a unified focus, creative tension will introduce additional chaos. Only after the focus is clear can the firm try to develop a strong momentum; only after momentum is established can it consider increasing the level of creative tension.

Providing Focus

The five conditions necessary for achieving a unified focus, the first level of organizational fit, are as follows. The strategy should be simple and clear, with a core concept; the priorities among its elements should be clear; supporting resources should be clearly allocated; it should stress striving consistently to improve; and it should match the corporate culture.

In Chapter 1 I introduced the core concept of strategy, whose purpose is to express concisely the strategy's specific content. I want to reemphasize the importance of the core concept here. If the basic ideas that underlie strategy are presented clearly, people in the organization will find it easier to understand the direction they are to take. When all parts of the organization share this understanding, they can make a unified effort. As each unit makes plans at its own level, the core concept can become its basic operating principle.

The core concept has to be simple but clear. If it is too complicated, it may be misunderstood; no matter how hard the strategist works to communicate the concept to the organization, the message will get distorted. Communication passes through a series of interpretations as it goes down through the organizational layers, so some misunderstanding is inevitable. Having a core concept is one way to lessen this problem. By presenting the strategy in a few phrases or key words, the strategist is more likely to put across the strategy at every level of the organization.

Nippon Electric Company (NEC) has used the slogan "computers and communication" as its core concept. This phrase has all the required attributes for successfully presenting a strategy. It tells everyone that the company's priority is on the melding of computer and telecommunications products and technology. Koji Kobayashi, the chief executive officer of NEC, said:

> Building bigger computers is not the only way to compete in the computer business. Since we have always been strong in telecommunications, we will continue to use that expertise in those product areas. We tell our organization that we should also deploy those advantages from the telecommunications area in computers as well. Rather than only working to build bigger computers, NEC should be working toward computer networks, deploying our telecommunications resources in this area. Once computers further penetrate our society, they will surely be tied into our communication networks. We at NEC have been working for many years to achieve that goal. (Imai et al., 1983)

Using this core concept, NEC put its highest priority on personal computers and took the largest market share in Japan. It has also boldly entered the field of integrated circuits, a technology that is indispensable for both communications equipment and computers. In this field NEC has become the second largest manufacturer in the world.

The second requirement for a unifying focus is to have clear-cut priorities. The organization must know which strategy elements are most important. Priorities have two important benefits: they avoid ambiguities, which invite communication failure, and they steer strategy away from the influence of internal politics.

No organization is single-minded in its outlook. There are always possibilities for conflict of interest, either within a work group or between groups. People naturally feel that the areas they know most about are most important. Each person will act in his own self-interest, which can lead to conflict. If a company's strategy does not include clear priorities, the individual units will simply set their own priorities, or "logrolling" between units will be the mechanism for setting them. This will result in a lack of integration in executing the strategy. It is easy to see the benefit of avoiding the ad hoc setting of priorities by having the strategist provide a clear set. This is especially important when a new strategy requires a very different set of priorities from those the firm is accustomed to. Without a clear emphasis on the new priorities, the organization will continue to operate under its old patterns and politics.

The deployment of resources, or a change in the deployment, can also help create a unified focus. A firm will allocate its resources in a way that is consistent with its strategy, so employees will understand the framework through changes in that allocation. If one important division continues to receive funds for product development during a recession, the organization knows that this division has top priority. If the firm uses the excuse of poor business performance to cut that division's product development budget along with others', members of the organization will doubt that the division really is central to the strategy. Kanebo, the Japanese textile manufacturer, did not cut back its research in cosmetics when its main product line, synthetic textiles, went into recession because of the rise in oil prices. If it had cut back on cosmetics, people in the organization would have doubted the firm's strategy of diversification. Kanebo would not have been able to sustain the organizational commitment necessary to develop this now-successful product line. Similarly, if Toray, another major Japanese textile firm, had used the recession as an excuse to cut back on research on composite-fiber products, it would never have developed its dominant worldwide position in that market. Allocation of resources communicates a great deal about the intent and direction of strategy.

A change in organizational structure, with its corresponding personnel changes, often means making changes in resource allocation. Misawa Homes used this mechanism to implement a new strategy. In 1975, in the aftermath of the oil shock, Misawa Homes, like all construction companies, was in deep trouble. It undertook a major organizational change to deal with that change in the environment. As *The Age of Masters* describes the change, "Misawa Homes made an unprecedented organizational reform on August 21, 1975. The company needed a major success to pull it out of the morass it was in. To do that, the company created a strategic action corps to develop new products . . . Two completely new organizations (The First and Second Production Divisions) were established" (Uchihashi, 1980b). The two new units were free to experiment. Staffed by people carefully selected from the research, manufacturing, and operations divisions of the company, the units were asked to work toward achievement of this single goal. Once the employees were informed of the reorganization and knew who was going to be assigned to these divisions, they understood that top management was determined to address the problem.

People in an organization watch what is going on carefully. When resources are reallocated, they quickly grasp the direction the strategist is taking. New personnel assignments, such as Misawa's new divisions staffed from all over the company, also give that message. The personnel changes informed everyone about management's intentions.

An organization cannot maintain a fast pace continually over a long period; the goal must be more modest: to perform a bit better and do it consistently for a long time. This will lead to excellent performance levels. Management will always work toward, and sometimes achieve, outstanding performance. When favorable environmental changes or miscalculations by competitors create the right conditions, a strategy that emphasizes doing a bit better will produce a stunning success. That success will have many long-lasting spillover effects. But management cannot expect the organization to make superb maneuvers all the time; there is no way to maintain the necessary tension for swift actions over a long time.

A more feasible goal is to do a little bit better all the time. It is the ability to stay one step above the competition that distinguishes successful companies from the rest. When each employee tries to be a cut above the competition, the firm will build up an invisible asset. This long-term goal has appeal for the people in the organization as well as top management. It is not that hard to be a little bit better; everyone can make that extra effort. Few people, however, can endure aspiring to be a lot better all the time. If it demands what only a few people can do, the strategy will not have a unified focus.

If possible, strategy should be within the bounds of the feelings, views, and values of the employees. Activities that clash with the corporate culture will be much harder to carry out. If the strategy forces people to undertake activities they feel unfit to do, they are unlikely to be effective. People will unconsciously implement a strategy in ways consistent with the corporate culture.

Hewlett Packard had always based its marketing on the technical superiority of its instruments and minicomputers. When the company entered the personal computer market, its sales and technical support people, who were used to dealing with customers who understood the technical jargon, had a hard time adjusting to a market in which consumers knew little about computers. The PC customer was intimidated rather than impressed with technical jargon, which had been an excellent marketing tool in other markets. This may be one reason Hewlett Packard has not been especially successful in this segment of the market.

If NEC, which sells earth stations for communications satellites, tried to attack Casio in the calculator market, the sales personnel would have to make substantial changes in the way they look at business. A calculator sale is measured in months, a satellite system in years. The sums of money involved are different by several orders of magnitude. The approach for winning sales from an African national communications company is different from that for selling to a large number of small-scale distributors and retail outlets. It is not that one type of sales expertise is harder to develop than the other. More than either know-how or product knowledge, values, and a feel for the market are the barriers.

Another reason to avoid a strategy that does not match the corporate culture is that it is much more difficult to get the organization to agree on how to implement such a strategy. Once this confusion sets in, it is difficult to make a unified effort. At the very least, it will take longer to create that unity.

I have discussed two reasons to avoid choosing a strategy that challenges the corporate culture. First, people will follow patterns of action that differ from those intended by the strategy, and, second, consensus will be harder to build. In the next section, however, I show that sometimes a strategist must ignore this advice to reach the next level of organizational fit. Still, without having first achieved this base of unified focus, the strategist will not dare to disturb this level of organizational fit.

Creating Momentum

To achieve momentum, a strategist must do four things: raise a "banner" to show the organization the core concept, make sure there are some small successes early on, have many people work together intensively on a single project, and pay attention to timing.

It has been said that an organization lives on dreams, that it needs more than financial incentives. If top management can get employees to feel that their personal dreams are tied to the organization's goals, its dreams, if you will, it can create high morale and achieve organizational momentum. If top management can *unfurl a banner in front of the organization,* pointing in the appropriate direction and showing a dream that workers can identify with, then the organization will pick up momentum. Toshihiko Yamashita of Matsushita put it this way: "Top management can have the best ideas and put out the greatest plans, but in the end, the result depends on people. If your organization is to be dynamic, the people in it have to become motivated and dynamic. How do you make that happen? You make the people feel that what they are doing is good for the society. Without that feeling, you will never be able to activate your organization" (Iizuka and Yamashita, 1984).

Momentum often comes from this type of ideal, a dream. Short-term, practical strategy of course has its place, but without something to look forward to, momentum cannot build. Distinguished leaders of great organizations have always loved festivals, occasions for unfurling the banner and emphasizing the organization's dream. When newspapers in the United States reported that Americans' confidence in the future of the country increased because of the pageantry and profits of the 1984 Olympics, they were reporting essentially this feature of festivals.

When managers known as turnaround experts come into a company that has been doing poorly for a long time, they try to breathe some life back into it. They often use the technique of unfurling a banner, creating a dream. Of course they have to tighten up loose management, but that is not enough. To regain momentum, a new dream of the future is necessary.

Turnaround experts use another technique: they try to give the organization a taste of success. A company that has been down for a long time has usually given up really trying. Unless the mood of defeatism is wiped out, nothing can be accomplished. The best medicine for malaise is a few small success stories. It really does not matter whether the successes have great significance; all that matters is that they occur, and people regain the feeling that "we can do it."

A small success can also be beneficial when a company enters a new area, when it may be hard to build consensus for the new policy. Arranging for a small success at an early stage will lessen resistance to the new enterprise and will show the organization that this strategic direction is appropriate. With greater acceptance, momentum will build faster. Logic means less to people in the organization than what is happening around them. If a strategy that is being questioned passes its initial test, even if the test is not a crucial one, momentum will build for its acceptance. Nothing convinces people like a success in the real world.

Motorola tried to get into the Japanese market for electronics equipment for many years. Then it decided to sell pagers, which tell executives of waiting phone calls, to the Japanese telecommunications monopoly, Nippon Telephone and Telegraph (NTT). Some might consider this a rather minor sale, of little meaning to a company the size of Motorola. But that sale told Motorola employees that the Japanese market could be cracked and increased their motivation for further efforts. Motorola trumpeted the accomplishment in full-page ads in American magazines, showing not just the Japanese consumer but also the U.S. market that it could succeed in Japan. Small successes are indeed valuable in developing strategy for a new market or situation.

Taio Paper, a successful company in Japan, moved into the field of printing papers in 1975. Taio's distribution system was revolutionary for that market: it chose to sell directly to the users instead of through the existing, multitiered distribution channel. To build organizational momentum for this unconventional policy, the company located the first two sales offices in areas where everyone knew that competition was keen. The executive vice president, Takao Ikawa, explained the decision: "It was hard to reach a consensus inside the company about building such an unconventional distribution network. We chose two places (Kanazawa and Shizuoka) that were considered very tough markets. If we could set up successfully in these difficult markets, we thought we could convince people that the new approach was correct.

Sure enough. After these two sales outlets succeeded, opposition died down, and the whole company moved to support the new distribution network" (Nomura Management School, 1981). It would not be wise to achieve such a small success at the expense of long-term strategy goals, of course, but sometimes, as with Taio's distribution system decision, the two goals are compatible. When a strategist can come up with the right idea, a small success can play an important role in creating momentum.

Momentum is more easily created when people understand each other and feel that they are all part of the larger organization. Working on a project with people from other sections of the company gives employees an insight into their objectives and ways of working and generates good feelings. For this reason a firm often tries to get as many people as possible to work on a particular project simultaneously. Understanding is increased, and top management can nurture a feeling that "we" are cooperating for the same organizational goals. Companies use various techniques to generate concerted action.

In the mid-1970s, when Mazda's sales were plummeting because of the failure of the Wankel rotary engine, the company assigned engineers to work with sales subsidiaries and dealers. The company felt that its survival depended on increased sales in the domestic market. Reassigning employees during the emergency made all sections of the firm aware of the short-term sales objectives. This move also had the unintended benefit, however, of giving different groups the experience of working together. After the crisis, Mazda engineers had an increased appreciation for customers, and the dealers had a more sophisticated understanding of the technical side of the business (Rohlen, 1983). Some companies use campaigns based on a particular theme, hoping that all the employees will consider the theme in light of their own work problems. Another method is to focus on one area to a greater extent than conventional wisdom suggests. Everyone will have to work together on the project (for example, being better in personal computers than any other electronics company).

The timing of a thrust for organizational momentum may determine its success. If the timing is wrong, no matter how well the strategist analyzes the environment and deploys his resources, the strategy may fail. Conversely, with the right timing, a strategy may succeed even with less than perfect environmental or resource fit. When an opportunity crops up to ride the momentum, a strategist may deliberately forgo environmental and resource fit to some extent. It is important to consider timing in the sequence of activities. The strategist should always be aware of organizational momentum as it develops so he can use it at key points to integrate strategy. Correct timing is important in all aspects of business strategy—meeting an increase in demand, parrying competitors' thrusts, accumulating resources—and the timing of momentum requires the same managerial attention.

Sustaining Creative Tension

The third level of fit is creative tension. One of the most serious problems an organization faces is complacency. Management must create the tension necessary to prevent complacency and put continuing pressure on the organization to avoid taking the easy way out. If it is carefully crafted, strategy can be used to achieve creative, forward-looking (as opposed to destructive) tension.

For this third level of organizational fit, the strategist must shake up the organization. If a bottle of salad dressing is allowed to settle, the oil and vinegar will separate and the spices will collect on bottom. Organizations are like that. Even if all the resources are in place, the strategist has to shake up the organization if she wants a well-mixed, zesty strategy. If the conditions leading to complacency are changed, the organization will be aimed at the next higher goal. Without tension, the leap to the next goal will not be possible. A strategy for developing and maintaining creative tension must introduce new elements into the employees' daily activities. Such a strategy must do the following: try to venture into new fields, reach for the limits of consensus, take an unbalanced approach to resource and environmental fit, and consciously select a strategy that does not match the corporate culture.

A strategist will first look for new products, new markets, or new elements of the operations mission to create tension. In each new undertaking, people in the organization have to face unknown situations and confront new problems. The new element should, of course, be consistent with the overall strategy. It should use accumulated resources or help develop or maintain environmental fit. Ideally, the experience should be transferable to other parts of the firm. To be the source of creative tension, however, a new element must be different from the organization's current pattern. One top manager, who felt that his staff was very set in its ways, said to them, "Do something new for me. I don't care if it has only a little effect; I don't care what the outcome will be. I just want you to do something new for its own sake!" Even in a less extreme situation, the creative tension created through entry into a new field is valuable.

To develop tension, a strategy should operate at the limits of organizational consensus. Organizations are very conservative; by nature they do not welcome anything new. Thus every new element has to be carefully integrated. If it is too different from what the firm is used to, integration will be impossible; if it is easily integrated, then it probably is not sufficiently new to create the desired tension. The appropriate pattern of consensus is illustrated in Figure 7–2.

Avoiding the two extremes is not easy; strategy must be within the range of consensus, but not too far within it. Acceptance should be barely attained, if the strategy is to create tension. There is an old Jewish saying, "If we have unanimous approval, we'd better take a second

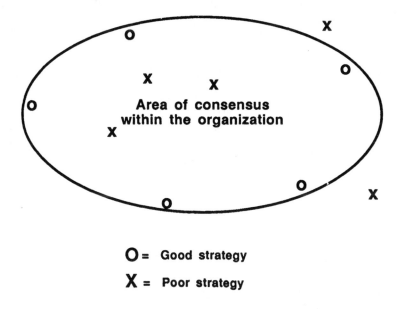

Figure 7–2. Strategies at the limits of consensus

look." If a strategy gets more than this hesitant approval, it is not leading the organization. If it gets no approval, its potential for leadership is wasted. If strategy errs in the other direction, however, and the leadership is afraid of introducing creative tension, new ideas will not be introduced fast enough to keep up with competitors. A barely achieved consensus is the best balance.

It is not unusual to encounter initially strong opposition to ultimately successful projects. This is what strategy is all about: convincing the organization against the conservative view of the majority. In 1974, in the middle of the economic adjustment to the first oil shock, Ushio Electric, a lamp manufacturer, got rid of a third of its products, those that were not expected to do well in the changed environment. Because there were no immediate replacements to fill the gap, naturally the organization did not accept the decision easily; there was strong dissent within the firm. Some of the objections were that the products were earning profits at that time, and that the high yen value was probably temporary. People felt that the policy would annoy established customers. Although each of these arguments was convincing, in the end the decision was made to scrap the products (Tokunaga, 1979b).

As the employees had anticipated, Ushio's profits from operations were only a third of the previous year's. But the company put employees from the scrapped product lines into sections that were developing new products, and after the initial shock, Ushio recovered quickly and soon was quite profitable. If it had aimed for more than this barely achievable consensus, these dramatic results would not have been possible. If it had dropped fewer products, the development of new products would have been delayed. The decision did more than free up resources for new products, however; it planted in people's minds a sense of urgency about new product development and marketing. The strategy generated the necessary creative tension for increased competitiveness.

The third way to introduce creative tension into the organization is through a strategy that does not totally fit the environment or the resources, that is, a *strategic imbalance*. Sometimes a short-term unbalanced strategy, by driving people to deal with the imbalance, creates and maintains long-term organizational fit.When an imbalance is introduced, the initial organizational reaction does not function well in the new situation. People are forced to work under conditions for which they are not prepared, which is not pleasant and will not have good results. This situation is a source of tension within the organization. But then the employees will try to find ways to correct this problem on their own. They must recognize that there is a problem before they can go after solutions. The strategist forces that recognition by introducing an unbalanced strategy.

Strategic imbalance must have an objective; people must understand why the firm is making them struggle. They must be shown that dealing with the imbalance will help the firm achieve its long-term goals, such as increased profits or higher levels of invisible assets that improve readiness to move into new areas. Casio's strategy for moving into integrated circuit design introduced resource imbalance in the early stages. The company started working in integrated circuits without having resources in that technology. In fact, it started with the intention of accumulating the technology. This introduced tension into the organization, to be sure, but that tension accelerated the accumulation of integrated circuits technology, which later became the core invisible asset of Casio's business.

An unbalanced strategy can also speed up decision making within the organization. The tension created by imbalance can put pressure on people to make necessary decisions. In such a tension-filled environment, people are less likely to put off a key decision or find excuses to delay.

Suntory's advance into the very competitive beer market provides a good example of the effect of unbalanced conditions on performance. The move created tension that resulted in a revitalization of the whole company. In working extra hard to sell small quantities of beer, the salespeople learned more about dealing with liquor stores and selling whiskey and more about what invisible assets they needed to accumulate.

The last method for introducing creative tension is to choose a strategy that does not fit the corporate culture. Again the strategist must walk a tightrope between an unbalanced strategy that introduces too much tension and one that does not generate the desired change in the corporate culture.

The first level of organizational fit required a unifying focus, and I said that without matching the corporate culture, it was impossible to build such a focus. It may seem strange to reverse myself at this third level, but what I am suggesting is that a firm occasionally may want to challenge its own culture. When the company is evolving and making some strategic leaps, it must choose strategies that are temporarily not in keeping with the corporate culture. The purpose of such an unbalanced strategy may be to change that culture. As with unbalanced strategies in the environment or resource areas, the rationale is that creative tension will generate transformation.

It may be too risky to choose an unbalanced strategy that influences the entire company; the tension level may get too high. Ideally, the strategy should initially affect only a portion of the operations, with the expectation that the effects will eventually reach all parts of the organization.

Taio Paper's strategy is a good example. The company, a manufacturer of newsprint, cardboard, and industrial papers, decided to enter the home tissue paper market in the late 1970s. At that time it had had only three years of experience in the field of printing papers, which depends on a strong marketing approach, as does the tissue paper market. Asked if it was not a bit presumptuous to enter the tissue paper field, given the company's lack of experience in this area, Takao Ikawa replied:

> There were many reasons for our move. It's a high value-added product, but what we really wanted was to change the mind set of our employees. For our company as a whole, we have to create a marketing orientation if we are to remain competitive. Still, our organization has not accepted this as yet. That's one of the reasons we decided to get into this household paper product line. If you are not marketing-oriented in this business, it will show up in performance. We hoped, by integrating household paper products into our product line, to create an atmosphere where workers could experience the importance of marketing orientation. The workers will also get a feel for exactly what is involved on an operational level in carrying out such a marketing-oriented business. (Nomura Management School, 1981)

But, one may ask, doesn't corporate culture determine strategy rather than vice versa? It is true that corporate culture dictates what strategy is appropriate, but the strategy can cause changes in the culture. Because corporate culture is largely determined by the environmental and competitive factors in the firm's field, a strategy that selects a new field will determine the corporate culture in the long run.

A change in corporate culture through strategy occurred at IBM. The company's personal computer strategy changed its approach in other computer areas as well. IBM's personal computer took control of this market only three years after it was introduced, a stunning success that no one expected. The development process for this product was quite inconsistent with IBM's corporate culture. Development teams were organized as though this were a venture capital project, and headquarters did not get involved in management. The microprocessor, the core of the PC, was purchased outside for the first time in IBM's history. Rather than develop its own software as had always been done, the group had outside companies develop it to their specifications. To help manufacturers and software writers develop products that would work with the PC, IBM made hardware and software specifications available, something it had seldom done before. To those who knew IBM well, these strategies seemed unthinkable. Yet the strategy was a success in the consumer market, where the customers were quite different from IBM's usual customers. As a result of this strategy, IBM became a more vital company and encouraged other venture capital projects (*Business Week,* Oct. 3, 1983).

These examples show that strategy can introduce a new factor into the corporate culture, just as customers and competitors can. Strategy can change people's daily activities, but it can also change their work and the values they hold. The result will be a new corporate culture to match the organization's new tasks.

Overextension and
Invisible Assets

In this chapter I will unify a theme I have emphasized throughout the book: that the strategist must achieve dynamic fit with the environment over time. To do that, the firm must transcend its current level of invisible assets. A dynamic imbalance of strategy, resources, and organization is necessary for a successful long-term strategy.

Defining Overextension

The conventional wisdom is that a firm should not take on more tasks than its resources allow. According to a Japanese saying, "A crab should dig a hole no bigger than he can hide in." In other words, the strategist should choose projects that are within the firm's area of expertise and appropriate to its skill level. A strategy should fit its level of resources and take advantage of its corporate culture. But as I have argued, resource fit and organizational fit both require that the firm, over the short term, consciously create deviations from these ideals of static fit. Long-term strategic fit, I suggested, arises from the dynamics of people working to bring the firm to the desired condition of fit or balance. If strategic fit is understood in this dynamic sense, it is clear that the conventional wisdom will not lead to development of the invisible assets required for dynamic strategic fit. The crab has to dig a bigger hole to create room for growth.

Conventional wisdom fails to be a good guide because it underestimates the role of growth and change in designing a strategy. A firm that intends to grow and change needs to prepare by accumulating invisible assets. If a firm digs itself into a narrow hole, like the seemingly wise crab, it will be limited in what it can do later. A firm's strategy sometimes should require stretching its invisible assets. An occasional struggle with fierce competition may be necessary. When a firm undertakes activities that call for more assets than it has, it is taking an overextension strategy.

Most firms that have grown successfully have used an overextension strategy at some key points in their development. I have cited Suntory's entry into beer, Casio's into logic chips, and Taio Paper's into household paper products. There is no guarantee that overextension will always succeed; in fact, many fail. But significant growth can hardly be expected unless a firm tries such a strategy.

One more example, that of Sumitomo Bank, will reinforce this point (Bronte, 1980). In 1979 its president, Ichiro Isoda, implemented a shakeup of the management structure. He hoped that this change would force the employees to acquire new skills. One goal of the reorganization was to better serve the financial requirements of large firms, whose deposit and borrowing requirements had been handled by separate departments, as was customary in all Japanese banks. Isoda consolidated deposits and borrowing for each firm in a single "relationships management" unit. Isoda also emphasized a substantial increase in the bank's commitment to international markets by presenting the international division as one of three main divisions. The number of sections in the international division tripled with the management changes.

The Japanese banking industry reacted with skepticism. Sumitomo was a well-run bank, but most analysts thought it would take a superman to run that kind of relationships management unit in Japan. It was the industry consensus that not even Sumitomo had enough personnel with international experience to pull off such an aggressive international strategy. Everyone believed Sumitomo had taken on more than it could handle. Isoda's response showed that he understood the importance of an appropriately timed overextension strategy. He felt that some day the bank would have to have relationships management and be more international, and he expected his people to grow into the new structure. Some people in Sumitomo Bank already had the necessary skills, and Isoda felt that more managers could develop them. He intended to build up the invisible assets the bank lacked (including human resources) as they gained experience in these new areas.

The firms that have followed overextension policies have had three things in common. First, they went into a new business area knowing that they could not do that business well at that time; second, they knew they would eventually have to get into that area; and third, they made sure that the invisible assets created with so much effort were used beyond the segment where they were initially accumulated. They made sure an internal billiard effect took place.

The overall growth of the postwar Japanese economy can be seen as a set of overextension strategies. The auto industry began production knowing that it could not make a competitive car for world markets, but that it had to develop the ability to do so. This overextension strategy had substantial spillover effects for the entire economy, clearly illustrating the potential of such a strategy.

In the budding Japanese computer industry of the 1950s, firms could easily have decided that they could never compete with giants like IBM in mainframe computers. If they had chosen strategies consistent with their low level of invisible assets, probably no Japanese firm would be in this industry today. Instead, six firms decided on an overextension strategy to stay in the mainframe business. Those six did not all succeed, but the industry as a whole grew tremendously. Just as in the automobile industry, the accumulated invisible assets formed the industrial base for other industries—integrated circuits and the whole gamut of electronics-based products that have revolutionized Japanese industry—and thus led to spillover effects throughout the economy.

Why Overextension Is Effective

Overextension must be done with a specific purpose. Management cannot just tell people to do anything that looks worth a try. Employees need to understand that the purpose of the strategy is to accumulate certain assets. Such a strategy can instill creative tension and help people learn by doing. When the strategist asks the organization to compete without all the necessary invisible assets, people are put in a state of great creative tension. I call this the "tension signal effect."

The "learning by doing" effect enables the firm to accumulate the necessary invisible assets to carry out future strategy in the course of its everyday operations. When a firm participates in a market in which there are strong competitive pressures, it gains a great deal of information as a result. The pressure-cooker atmosphere of such markets provides high-quality feedback. The resources accumulated under these difficult conditions are usually sturdy.

The firm's invisible assets are no more or less than the accumulated efforts of everyone in the organization. Creative tension can increase the level of effort and make sure that it is pointed in the proper direction. When everyone works to reach a stated goal, the focused effort is sure to produce more significant results than uncoordinated, individual efforts.

Resources accumulated in these difficult conditions tend to be sturdy, like plants that have survived the strong winter winds. The human invisible assets of the firm must be well rooted and strong to survive the harsh winds of competition. You do not find such hardy plants very often in a nursery; the same goes for hardy invisible assets. A firm cannot buy well-developed invisible assets in the marketplace, nor can it set up its own protected "nursery" in-house where its people are sheltered from competition. The resources must be exposed to the harsh competitive environment to grow strong, and an overextension strategy can be the best way to do this.

One reason to take an overextension strategy is to get a head start in an area the firm intends to enter later. The invisible assets acquired in an early attempt, through tension and crisis, become the driving force as the company becomes competitive in that field. There may also be several types of spillover effects. The resources developed through an overextension strategy may increase the firm's competitive position in other areas. Or the tension created may energize the whole organization, allowing it to grow into new areas. This is what a dynamic imbalance of strategy, resources, and organization is all about.

Supporting Conditions

When an overextension policy is suggested, the first reaction often is that without the necessary backup, such a policy may be too dangerous in the face of ferocious competition. Large costs may have to be incurred right away if this strategy is to succeed. Certain conditions should be present to make a favorable outcome more likely. These conditions are: careful day-to-day measures for accumulating invisible assets, protection during the initial turbulence of the overextension period, determination to carry through, adequate financial support, and strong leadership from top management.

The first point emphasizes that the accumulation of invisible assets must be carefully integrated into the firm's activities in the overextended area. For example, the firm may spot an area where it can accumulate some needed invisible assets. It then must find ways to concentrate on this accumulation. Perhaps the firm has had outside firms control parts of the operations mission, but if that operation is important in accumulating invisible assets, it must now control this aspect within the firm, as Casio did with integrated circuit design. It may have to assign top people to that area to speed up the accumulation process. Later, these people will carry the invisible assets with them to other parts of the firm.

A firm that tries to compete without the necessary invisible assets may be in a weak position, so the second important condition is to have other invisible assets that will provide some protection during this vulnerable period. For example, Suntory's experience in advertising turned out to be a valuable invisible asset when it entered the beer market. And the Japanese government ban on direct investment by foreign car makers after World War II was a strong asset for the auto industry. Without resources to support the strategy, the firm may become totally overextended.

Third, the company has to be willing to carry through a project that will create resources usable in other fields, but only after a long struggle. If the firm gives up, all the potential gains will vanish. Sony did not give up when its initial attempt to enter the color television market failed. It went back to the drawing board and came out with the Trinitron one-gun picture tube, which swept the market a few years later.

Sufficient financial support is the next necessary supporting condition. Overextension is an investment in invisible asset accumulation, but there may be losses in the first few years. Thus, the company must be willing to stake the initial investment. Financial support is most likely to be available when the firm's core business is doing well. Overextension during that period has a better chance for success. When the main business is already in a pinch, overextension is not advisable.

The fifth supporting condition is strong leadership. Since overextension is inherently risky, people may resist its implementation. The senior management has to take a risky idea and get everyone in the organization to move in the right direction. Management must be strong yet attentive to the strategy. It is no accident that the four firms I cited earlier as examples of successful overextension strategy—Suntory, Casio, Sumitomo, and Taio Paper—all had strong leadership.

Some might argue that overextension can succeed only when the economy is growing quickly. I believe this is fallacious. When the economy is growing very fast, unquestionably a poorly conceived overextension may look like a success. The firm may not have to pay a price for its miscalculations. But if even a poorly conceived strategy can make money, the firm could have found more profitable uses for its invisible assets. However, when the economy is growing slowly, an overextension strategy can be even more important. At such a time people in the organization may begin to believe that no growth opportunities are left and may become complacent. Yet even in a slow-growing industry, there is always potential for growth; for example, the 3M Company developed scores of new products over the years in a relatively stable, industrial goods industry. An overextension strategy can force a firm to seek out such opportunities.

Recently, slow economic growth has been accompanied by two other trends that make an overextension strategy more desirable: rapid change in technology and increasing internationalization of world economies and markets. A firm's current portfolio of invisible assets is unlikely to fit this changing environment. With technology and global markets changing so quickly, a strategist cannot sit back and wait for assets to be ready before making a competitive move. Companies that anticipate the future level of invisible assets can reap ample rewards in such a slow-growing but fast-changing environment by pursuing an aggressive overextension strategy. The question is not whether to try such a strategy, but rather what kind of overextension best fits this environment.

Dynamic Imbalance

The logic of dynamic imbalance is not limited to the successful applications cited here from business. It is universal. To see the parallels in other economic areas, consider Albert Hirschman's (1967) comments on economic development. Hirschman, who observed and analyzed development projects in less-developed countries, pointed out that success in such projects resulted from overextension. Hirschman broke down the projects into two types: *trait-making* and *trait-taking*. A trait here refers to the milieu in which a development project is undertaken (for example, the political system, culture, education, technology, and infrastructure). In a trait-taking project those systems are unchangeable; the project must be designed with those systems as given.

In a trait-making project, on the other hand, the systems are not sufficient for the project to succeed initially, but the project tries to create the necessary traits as it progresses. Over the course of the project the traits must change so that the project can ultimately succeed. If an underdeveloped country undertakes only trait-taking projects, it may remain underdeveloped, unable to pull out of the existing conditions. If it undertakes safe projects, it never develops the infrastructure required for change. If the government contemplates a project that needs more advanced structures, it finds that it does not have the resources, so it rejects the project. For example, in a country where people are not accustomed to working according to a strict schedule, a project that conforms to that custom will not help the people change their work habits. For a short period the project may run smoothly, yet, that smooth operation will not meet the goal of development, transforming work habits.

There are always labor pains when a country chooses a trait-making project because it creates great pressures within the society. At the same time, such an approach provides an opportunity for learning the trait. Perhaps less-developed countries should more often be equipped with the most modern equipment, contrary to the conventional wisdom of using machines that fit the local conditions. Machines in modern plants require efficient production planning and a high level of knowledge at the workshop level. The pressure of having such machines can push people to acquire new attitudes and skills.

Overextension and trait-making are similar in that both focus on the development of dynamism created from an imbalance between the strategy (project) and the resource or organization (trait). Two characteristics of an overextension strategy generate dynamism: first, it destroys complacency, and second, it creates dynamic synergy. There is creative tension within the organization, and everyone benefits from learning by doing. Dynamic imbalance can revitalize a firm or a country and allow it to respond to a changing environment.

A firm should introduce new overextension strategies periodically. After introducing a shock of overextension, the firm must wait until balance is almost reestablished, then introduce another overextension strategy. Strategy will zigzag between balance and imbalance. Remember that the goal of an overextension strategy is to accumulate invisible assets to be in dynamic fit with the environment. If the strategy is successful, balance will eventually be restored, and the overextension will cease to exist. Then it is time to begin a new overextension.

Repeating this cycle is a necessary condition for growth and prosperity, but it is not a sufficient condition. Not all overextensions are chosen intentionally. Some may result from miscalculations of the resources required for a given strategy. But even an unintended overextension can still create the dynamism necessary for growth, if management reacts quickly.

Koji Kobayashi, chief executive officer of Nippon Electric, spoke to this issue:

> Companies that look unstable are the most stable in the long run; companies that look stable, the most unstable. This is seemingly paradoxical. I've felt this for a long time, ever since I first took a look at American corporate performance in the early 1950s. People in certain companies are always complaining about something. "Competition is tough"; "I wonder how long it will take to make some money on this project"; "Interest rates are sky high"; "Markets are forcing us to sell our products too cheaply." The troubles spill out. These are the "unstable companies," or so it seems. These same companies, however, are always trying to do something about these problems before they go from bad to worse. Thus, things seem to get better over time; the companies never get themselves into really dire straits. Just about the time they think things may be getting a bit less unstable, however, something happens to keep them on their toes. A new competitor enters the market; market conditions turn against the firm. The firm again has to seek ways to improve the situation. The pattern is repeated over and over.
>
> Contrast this with another set of companies, seemingly more stable. These companies can make money without exerting a great deal of effort. Workers feel fortunate to work for such a good company; management can take it easy. There is no worry about the company's position here. Unfortunately, such a situation never lasts. Both "stable" and "unstable" companies must face up to environmental changes sooner or later. The pattern of change is shown as the dashed diagonal line in the chart [Figure 8–1].

While an "unstable" company complains a lot about these changes, it is constantly trying to find solutions to problems as they come along. The path of this strategic change in shown by the zigzag line on the chart.

The seemingly fortunate company does not move with the times, maintaining its stable pattern of operations. The pattern is shown in the lower line in the chart. Eventually, these environmental changes become too great to be ignored. Then this seemingly stable firm has to make a major move, but neither the management nor the workers know how to deal with this kind of problem. Without knowing what was coming, the company could face bankruptcy in this situation. (Kobayashi, 1980)

Growth never occurs smoothly within a firm. As strategy, invisible assets, and the organization continually change, the balance among the various elements will not always be maintained. There may be a temporary glut of resources or too much of one kind. At other times, seemingly essential resources will be lacking. In the organization ten-

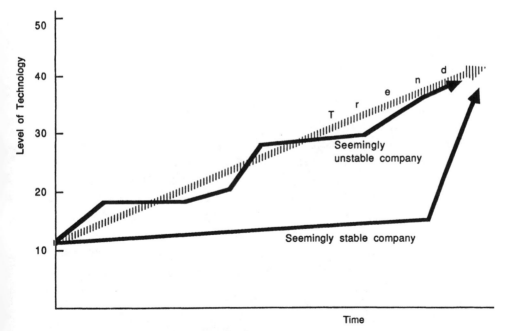

Figure 8–1. Technology trends and zigzag development

sion may reach a peak, then be followed by a period of relative relaxation. Strategy may be broad at times, extremely focused at others. All of these elements follow a zigzag path. Long-term strategy must follow this zigzag path if it is to fit the changing environment and the firm's continuing growth. This is how dynamic imbalance works.

"Fit" connotes balanced, stable conditions. But instead of ending with an emphasis on balance and on tight matching of strategy to environment, I end with an appeal for *imbalance,* a call for overextension in both strategy and invisible assets. The optimal path for growth is a zigzag, not a straight line.

It may seem contradictory to move from balance to imbalance, but according to my definition of strategic fit, the contradiction ceases to exist.

Previous studies of strategy have put too much emphasis on the environment, leading to a rather narrow economic analysis of strategy issues. These studies have relied on analyses of markets and of competitors, as well as current assets and technology. There is no room in these analyses for overextension; it does not fit into their logic, and they cannot integrate the benefits of dynamic imbalance.

In my theory, on the other hand, overextension is a natural element of logical strategy. This approach is also capable of incorporating dynamic imbalance. Without neglecting the more conventional economic elements of strategic analysis, I argue that invisible assets and human organizational factors are central to this analysis. It is not that the economic elements are unimportant, but that these two additional factors deserve equal emphasis. Strategy involves more than influencing the *external* environment of the firm. Just as important, it revolves around *internal* elements—resources and organization. Unless a firm's strategies include both types of elements, they will be too narrowly focused.

The messages of this book can be summed up as follows: strategy has a logic, and invisible assets, based on information, are important for all corporate activities, especially strategy. By logic, I do not mean just a one-dimensional economic logic, but a logic that is broad enough to include the human elements as well. I have used three sets of logic: conventional economic logic, the logic of invisible assets, and the logic of human psychology. It is important to view the world of business from all three perspectives.

In Pursuit of
Strategic Thinking

The Chinese strategist Sun Tzu once said:

> There are not more than five musical notes, yet the combinations of these five give rise to more melodies than can ever be heard. There are not more than five primary colors, yet in combination they produce more hues than can ever be seen. There are not more than five cardinal tastes—sour, acrid, salt, sweet, bitter—yet combinations of them yield more flavors than can ever be tasted.
>
> In battle, however, there are not more than two methods of attack—the direct and the indirect; yet these two in combination give rise to an endless series of maneuvers. (Sun Tzu [Clavell], 1983)

Just as a few basic elements combine to create innumerable variations in Sun Tzu's thought, so do a few basic points of corporate strategy form the basis for countless variations. Departing from the analytical framework of the rest of the book, I will review several key words that always come up in discussions of successful strategies. A common characteristic of good strategy is that the essential points have been well thought out. The seven essential points, or key words, for strategic thinking are: differentiation, concentration, repercussion, timing, organizational momentum, imbalance, and combination.

Differentiation

To build a successful strategy, a firm must differentiate itself from its competitors either in the marketing, products, price, and supplemental services or in efficiency of production and distribution, achieved through the choice of plant location, for example, or through lower labor costs. The variations are endless.

Differentiation can mean doing a better job than the competitors in similar operations, or it can mean creating a different product in a different environment. Finding the right niche or segment by developing a product that defines a new market can reduce competition. Since any market is quite heterogeneous, aiming at a different segment can set a firm apart. Successful differentiation results from the allocation of resources accumulated over the years in patterns that distinguish the firm from its competitors.

It is the consumers, however, who make the final decision on the success of a firm's differentiation efforts.

Concentration

An obviously important aspect of strategy is the concentration of corporate resources on certain products; on particular markets, functions, or operations; or on organizational efforts. In general terms, concentration means setting priorities. What portion of the bundle of customer desires should the firm focus on—pricing, product quality, or services? In each case priorities must be set for the use of the corporation's resources.

Focusing on the resources that are different from those of the competition also helps differentiate the firm. Once a concentration strategy has been worked out, the areas on which the firm has not concentrated may benefit from the repercussion effects. A key to successful resource concentration is the creation of positive ripple effects. When a firm succeeds after concentrating its efforts on one product, this success creates trust and confidence, not just among consumers, but also within the entire organization. A concerted effort thus generates a sense of unity within the firm and strengthens its commitment to the strategy.

Repercussions

Repercussion effects occur when the success of one strategic activity leads to other possibilities for the future. The success of a first product builds customer confidence and demand for the next product. Technology developed in one product area turns out to be useful in other areas as well. A success in a narrow market segment leads to potential markets in wider sectors. Capital investment at the right time enables full use of facilities, and the resulting relaxation of capital requirements makes it easier to make the next investment. A small success early in the game gives the organization confidence. Repercussions ensure that the benefits from concentration are not frittered away. Success through concentration creates a basis for repercussions. A well-executed strategy that has repercussion effects can be used as a lever to parlay a small stock of resources into a significant economic return.

Timing

The importance of timing cannot be stressed too much. A firm should always try to introduce a new product one step ahead of its competitors. The strategist should try to gauge changes in consumer desires accurately and find out what might be holding back their demand, then break the bottleneck with new products or services.

Offering a service that consumers have not yet demanded will not work, simply because it has been marketed too early. A firm must carefully prepare to implement a strategy, but it should not implement it until the time is ripe. And even without complete preparation, if the timing is correct, a strategy may be successful. Deciding when to launch a strategy is a key to its fate. This judgment must take into consideration corporate resource accumulation and organizational momentum.

A good illustration is capital investment. When capital expansion is not timed to coincide with an increase in demand, the company suffers multiple damages; idle plants reduce investment returns, and the pressure of inventory investment increases, aggravating cash flow problems and delaying other important investments in research and development, sales, or employee training. Idle plants reduce the morale of workers, and as a result the product quality suffers. Even worse, the company may feel compelled to put idle facilities and equipment to work. It may order more supplies, incurring further loss when products do not sell, or it may introduce a product for which there is insufficient demand. The low rate of return from an idle plant is not as serious as the detrimental ramifications resulting from bad timing.

Momentum

Organizational momentum results from repercussion effects and from concentration. Good timing also increases a firm's momentum. If it has a small success, the organization picks up momentum. If it then loses momentum, the benefits of repercussion may be lost.

Strategists have to make sure that momentum does not take the firm in the wrong direction, however. If a company succeeds in a particular market because of a short-term rise in demand, it may divert resources to that market. That diversion, however, may not be consistent with the long-term strategy. Once the momentum has been set in the wrong direction, there is no easy way to stop it. From a strategic viewpoint, the firm may have to kill the momentum or reforge it to be consistent with the long-term goals.

Imbalance

A strategy for creating and maintaining momentum and tension within the organization cannot always be smooth and orderly. An unbalanced strategy that shakes up an organization is best for its long-term health. The firm should have periods when its resources and talents are not in balance with its current strategy. The organization should not remain in equilibrium for very long, or it will lose momentum. When balance seems to be returning, strategy should introduce the next imbalance to stimulate people's thinking and encourage learning. A firm finds its long-term pattern of growth through a series of zigzags.

Combination

Creating a market, product, or resource portfolio requires combining various business elements. The resulting portfolio benefits—complement and synergy effects—are well known. Existing portfolio elements may suggest new combinations. Japanese electronics firms took two existing products, the tape recorder and the transistor radio, and combined them to create the radio cassette recorder. A unified combination of corporate resources can give the firm a substantial competitive edge in product differentiation.

The whole can be greater than the sum of its parts. The value of a particular business element can rise substantially when it is combined with other resources or products. Combination in strategy means tapping the potential benefits of interdependence among the firm's resources. Each step in the process has the potential to develop a whole new aspect of a firm's strategy. Selling personal computers, for instance, requires developing production and technical capacity. To achieve that capacity, a firm must simultaneously develop operations and software. The automated production line may work well to produce some peripherals as well, and the firm is then able to sell a system rather than just the central processing unit. Meanwhile, the firm and its customers discover new uses for the personal computer that require yet more changes in production and technical capacity.

Each of these relatively simple combinations builds toward a more complex overall strategy. The final framework may seem to be a complex web of relationships, but it can be understood as an accumulation of simpler combinations. The more effective the firm is in dealing with these combinations, the better its strategy will look.

The various types of strategic logic discussed here are based on the idea of fit, which is really the same logic as in the network of combinations. The overall strategy, in all its complexity, results from these basic combinations. Even the list of key words for strategy falls under the heading of combination. The key words should not be considered separately; they should be used in combinations: concentration and differentiation, timing and differentiation, repercussion and momentum. In that sense, combination is really the key word of these key words.

Works Cited

Amada, Isamu. 1979. Big profits with an inimitable selling system. (In Japanese.) *Nikkei Business,* June 4, pp. 32–35.

Bellew, Patricia. 1984. Osborne tries for a comeback in computers. *Wall Street Journal,* Oct. 12, p. 33.

Bronte, Stephen. 1980. Sumitomo's hunger for profits. *Euromoney,* September, pp. 29–49.

Business Week. May 17, 1982. Why Timken's stability will save its bottom line. Pp. 107–108.

Business Week. Oct. 3, 1983. How the PC changed the way IBM thinks.

Business Week. Oct. 12, 1983. Fuji Photo: Sharpening its image in the U.S. as it develops new products.

Bylinsky, Gene. 1981. The Japanese chip challenge. *Fortune,* Mar. 23, pp. 115–122.

Conte, Christopher. 1984. Charging bias, airlines ask CAB to change reservation systems at American, United. *Wall Street Journal,* Feb. 9, p. 29.

Hayes, Thomas C. 1984. Trilogy drops wafer scale chip. *New York Times,* Aug. 10, p. D1.

Hirschman, Albert O. 1967. *Development projects observed.* Washington, D.C.: Brookings.

Hotel and Restaurant Weekly. Dec. 2, 1977. Skylark. (In Japanese.) Pp. 50–55.

Iizuka, Akio, and Toshihiko Yamashita. 1984. *Thoughts on management.* (In Japanese.) Tokyo: Kanki.

Imai, Kenichi, et al. 1983. The formulation and development of NEC's "C and C" strategy. (In Japanese.) *Business Review,* August, pp. 86–96.

Industrial Bank of Japan, Center for Small Business Research. 1979. *Markets for smaller firms.* (In Japanese.) Tokyo: Diamond.

Itoh, Masatoshi. 1980. My practical management style. (In Japanese.) *Toyo Keizai,* May 10, pp. 104–107.

Japan Economic Journal. Mar. 1, 1983. Nestlé to set up R and D center to develop products suited to the Japanese market. P. 18.

Kobayashi, Koji. 1980. *C and C is Japan's wisdom.* (In Japanese.) Tokyo: Simul Press.

Lehner, Urban. 1982. Japanese market, once hostile to U.S., is opening to imports. *Wall Street Journal,* May 12, pp. 1, 24.

Michida, Kunio. 1979. Ricoh's return to cameras. (In Japanese.) *President,* December, pp. 114–121.

Misawa, Chiyoji. 1984. Comment by Mr. Chiyoji Misawa of Misawa Homes. (In Japanese.) *Nikkei Business,* Mar. 5, p. 156.

Mito, Setsuo. 1977. Challenge for strategic growth. (In Japanese.) *President,* January, pp. 74–81.

Moriya, Masanori. 1978. *Industrial technology.* (In Japanese.) Tokyo: Toyo Keizai.

Murray, Geoffrey. 1984. Braun: Cutting into Japan's shaver market. *Journal of Japanese Trade and Industry,* March/April, pp. 44–46.

Nagata, Kohei. 1979. Case study: Sekisui House. (In Japanese.) *Nikkei Business,* Mar. 12, pp. 116–121.

Nagata, Kohei, and Takuzo Tokunaga. 1979. Casio moves into new fields with its calculator technology. (In Japanese.) *Nikkei Business,* July 16, pp. 44–48.

Nakagawa, K. 1983. *The development of the Japanese semiconductor industry.* (In Japanese.) Tokyo: Diamond.

Nakamura, Tsuneya. 1984. Product diversification to keep sales growing. *Japan Times,* Mar. 12.

Nihon Keizai Shimbun. Aug. 13, 1984. Sony to increase 3.5-inch floppy production capacity. (In Japanese.) P. 7.

Nikkei Business. July 3, 1978. Kao. (In Japanese.) Pp. 62–65.

Nikkei Business. Oct. 9, 1978. Chofu Engineering. (In Japanese.) Pp. 132–135.

Nikkei Business. July 16, 1979. Hakubi. (In Japanese.) P. 86.

Nikkei Business. Mar. 22, 1982. Developing strategies for advanced technology: TDK. (In Japanese.) P. 186.

Nikkei Business. Mar. 22, 1982. Developing strategies for advanced technology: Fujitsu. (In Japanese.) P. 187.

Nomura Management School. 1981. Taio Paper Case A. (In Japanese.)

Oka, Takashi. A positive management style takes root in Japan. 1982. *Christian Science Monitor,* Dec. 24, p. 11.

Rohlen, Thomas P. 1983. The Mazda turnaround. *Journal of Japanese Studies* 9: 219–264.

Shimura, Noriaki. 1979. Comment by Mr. Shimura of Casio. (In Japanese.) *Nikkei Business,* Oct. 8, pp. 160–162.

Stearns, Jeff. 1983. Asahi Glass diversification drive stresses research. *Asian Wall Street Journal Weekly,* Sept. 26.

Steele, Lowell. 1983. Managers' misconceptions about technology. *Harvard Business Review,* November-December, pp. 133–140.

Sun Tzu [Clavell]. 1983. *The Art of War.* New York: Delacorte.

Tabuchi, Setsuya. 1984. Financial revolution. (In Japanese.) *Business Review,* March, pp. 59–65.

Takahashi, Arataroh. 1980. *What I learned from Konosuke Matsushita.* (In Japanese.) Tokyo: Jitsugyo no Nihonsha.

Takayanagi, Kenjiro. 1980. Interview with Mr. Takayanagi of Victor. (In Japanese.) *Nikkei Business,* Mar. 10, pp. 133–134.

Tokunaga, Takuzo. 1979a. Toyo Sash's product concept. (In Japanese.) *Nikkei Business,* Feb. 26, pp. 133–135.

Tokunaga, Takuzo. 1979b. Ushio Electric looks to the future with a major product line shakeup. (In Japanese.) *Nikkei Business,* Mar. 26, pp. 51–52.

Toyo Keizai. July 7, 1979. Nikon vs. Canon: The struggle to stay on top. (In Japanese.) Pp. 76–80.

Toyo Keizai. Dec. 15, 1979. Komatsu Forklift: Independent management now reflected in higher profits. (In Japanese.) Pp. 75–77.

Toyo Keizai. Aug. 27, 1983. Accumulating experience with a losing beer. (In Japanese.) Pp. 80–83.

Treece, James B., et al. 1985. How Kodak is trying to move Mt. Fuji. *Business Week,* Dec. 2, p. 62.

Uchihashi, Katsuto. 1980a. *Masters of management.* (In Japanese.) Tokyo: Sankei.

Uchihashi, Katsuto. 1980b. *The age of masters.* (In Japanese.) Tokyo: Sankei.

Yamasaki, A. 1978. *Renown's management system.* (In Japanese.) Tokyo: President.

Yamasaki, Kiyoshi, and Shigeo Takeda. 1976. *Foreign firms in Japan.* (In Japanese.) Tokyo: Kyuikusha.

General References

Andrews, Kenneth R. 1980. *The concept of corporate strategy,* rev. ed. Homewood, Ill.: Irwin.

Ansoff, H. Igor. 1965. *Corporate strategy.* New York: McGraw-Hill.

Henderson, Bruce D. 1979. *Henderson on corporate strategy.* Cambridge, Mass: Abt Associates.

Hirschman, Albert O. 1958. *The strategy of economic development.* New Haven: Yale University Press.

Hofer, Charles W., and Dan E. Schendel. 1978. *Strategy formulation: Analytical Concepts.* St. Paul, Minn.: West Publishing.

Levitt, Theodore. 1978. *Marketing for business growth.* New York: McGraw-Hill.

Ohmae, Ken-ichi. 1983. *The mind of the strategist.* New York: McGraw-Hill.

Penrose, Edith T. 1959. *The theory of the growth of the firm.* New York: Wiley.

Porter, Michael E. 1980. *Competitive strategy.* New York: Free Press.

Rosenberg, Nathan. 1976. *Perspectives on technology.* Cambridge: Cambridge University Press.

Yoshihara, Hideki, Akimitsu Sakuma, Hiroyuki Itami, and Tadao Kagono. 1981. *Diversification strategies of Japanese firms.* (In Japanese.) Tokyo: Japan Economic Journal.

Index